ORGANIC SELF-CARE:

A RADICAL GUIDE TO MENTAL WELLNESS

Introduction: The Call to Care

Overview of radical self-care as an act of revolution and resilience

In a relentless hustle world and gig economy, self-care is easily dismissed as indulgent or self-centered. But organic self-care challenges this narrative, asserting that caring for oneself is not only a natural necessity but also a revolutionary act. It reclaims the fundamental truth that wellness and wholeness are inherent rights, not privileges reserved for the few.

Radical self-care is rooted in the understanding that our well-being is deeply intertwined with the social, political, and cultural systems we navigate daily. It recognizes that systemic oppression, economic inequality, and historical injustices often leave individuals, particularly marginalized communities, drained and disconnected from their inner core. By prioritizing our mental, physical, and emotional health, radical self-care resists the structures that seek to exploit and dehumanize us.

Angela Davis, a profound thinker and activist, framed self-care as a form of resistance. In her view, choosing to nurture oneself in a society that commodifies human beings is a bold act of defiance. To care for one's mind, body, and spirit is to reject the notion that we exist solely for labor or external validation. It's a declaration that we deserve rest, joy, celebrations and dignity—irrespective of our circumstances or progress of the struggle.

Resilience lies at the heart of radical self-care. It's not about escaping life's challenges but rather nurturing the strength to face them with clarity and courage. Resilience means recognizing our capacity to heal and grow, even in the face of adversity. James Baldwin's writings often reflect this spirit. He taught us that acknowledging our pain and struggle is the first step toward transforming them. Radical self-care, then, becomes a vehicle for this transformation, empowering us to rise above our trials and find meaning within them.

But radical self-care goes beyond individual well-being; it's also deeply communal. When we care for ourselves, we create a ripple effect that extends to our relationships, our communities, and the world at large. Carl Jung's concept of individuation—the process of becoming whole—suggests that personal growth inevitably contributes to collective harmony. By addressing our internal wounds, we become better equipped to support and uplift others, fostering a cycle of care and connection.

Moreover, radical self-care is a deliberate act of reclaiming time and space for what truly matters. In his work, Jordan Peterson emphasizes the importance of responsibility and order in achieving a meaningful life. Radical self-care aligns with this principle by urging us to take ownership of our well-being, set boundaries, and prioritize activities that nourish our minds and bodies. It's about designing a life that reflects our values and aspirations rather than succumbing to external pressures.

At its core, radical self-care is a practice of self-awareness and intentionality. It asks us to confront our inner world honestly—to examine our fears, desires, and beliefs. This introspection can be challenging, but it's also liberating. It enables us to uncover the root causes of our struggles and to address them with compassion and resolve. In doing so, we reclaim our agency and reaffirm our worth. When applied in a collective, it allows for 'constructive' self criticism on top of constructive criticism of others.

In a society that thrives on performative culture, disconnection, and clout, radical self-care is nothing short of revolutionary. It challenges us to imagine a world where rest, joy, comfort, celebrations and healing are not luxuries but norms. It calls us to break free from cycles of overconsumption and to cultivate a life of abundance and balance. And it reminds us that caring for ourselves is not selfish but essential—a necessary step in building a more just and compassionate world.

As you embark on this journey of radical self-care, remember that it's not a one-time act but an ongoing commitment. It's a process of learning, unlearning, and evolving. And in choosing this path, you join a legacy of individuals who have dared to prioritize their well-being in the face of adversity.

Angela Davis on self-care as a political act

Angela Davis, a towering figure in the realms of radical activism and academia, has long emphasized the interconnectedness of self-care and the fight for social justice. For Davis, self-care is not merely a personal indulgence but a deliberate, political act of resistance against oppressive systems. This frame of thinking reshapes the narrative around care, highlighting its role as both a personal and collective necessity.

Davis's advocacy for self-care arose from her lived experiences as an activist and organizer. Her involvement in civil rights movements, her imprisonment, and her lifelong commitment to fighting systemic racism and inequality have shown her the toll that sustained activism can take on individuals. In this context, self-care becomes a survival strategy—a way to maintain the stamina required for long-term resistance. By nurturing one's physical, emotional, and mental health, activists and organizers can sustain their efforts without succumbing to burnout or despair.

At the heart of Davis's philosophy is the recognition that self-care is inherently political because it challenges the exploitative demands of capitalist systems. These systems often prioritize profit over people, valuing individuals only for their productivity. By choosing to care for ourselves, we reject this dehumanizing logic. We affirm our intrinsic worth, independent of what we produce or achieve in society. This act of affirmation is particularly powerful for marginalized communities, who are often denied access to rest days, paid leave and rejuvenation.

Davis also highlights the communal dimensions of self-care. She argues that caring for oneself enables individuals to better care for their communities. This interconnectedness transforms self-care from a solitary act into a collective one, fostering networks of mutual support and resilience. In this way, self-care becomes a building block for solidarity, ensuring that movements for justice and human rights remain vibrant and sustainable.

Furthermore, Davis juxtapositions self-care within the broader framework of revolutionary change. She draws parallels between personal healing and societal transformation, suggesting that the two are deeply intertwined. Just as individuals must confront and heal from personal trauma, societies must address and rectify systemic injustices. Self-care, therefore, is not an escape from activism but an integral part of it. It equips individuals with the clarity, strength, and compassion needed to envision and create a more equitable world.

Angela Davis's insights challenge us to reimagine self-care as an act of empowerment and resistance. By prioritizing our well-being, we not only reclaim our humanity but also contribute to the collective struggle for justice. Her message is a reminder that the personal and the political are inseparable—and that in caring for ourselves, we take a crucial step toward caring for the world.

Why this book matters: bridging the gap between peoples struggles and their self-renewal

In today's world, countless individuals are grappling with the weight of systemic pressures, personal challenges, and the relentless demands of a capitalist world. Amid these struggles, the pursuit of self-renewal often feels out of reach, relegated to the realm of luxury or unattainable ideals. This book seeks to deconstruct that misconception, offering an organic roadmap for bridging the gap between adversity and holistic well-being.

Why does this matter? Because radical self-care is not merely a self-help trend; it is a lifeline. It acknowledges the profound impact that systemic inequalities and personal hardships have on our mental, emotional, and physical health. For marginalized communities, who bear the brunt of these injustices, self-care becomes an urgent necessity rather than an optional practice. This book aims to meet readers where they are, to have empathy, offering practical tools and compassionate guidance to help them reclaim their power and renew their spirits.

The connection between struggle and self-renewal is both personal and universal. Struggles, whether rooted in systemic oppression, personal trauma, or everyday triggers, can leave us feeling depleted and disconnected from ourselves. But within these struggles lies the potential for transformation. Organic self-care offers a way to harness this potential, turning pain into purpose and adversity into growth.

This book matters because it challenges the pervasive narrative that self-care is selfish or superficial. By framing self-care as an act of resistance and renewal, it underscores its vital role in fostering individual and collective well-being. It draws inspiration from the teachings of Angela Davis, James Baldwin, Carl Jung, and Jordan Peterson, weaving their insights into a comprehensive guide for navigating life's challenges with courage and clarity.

For those who feel overwhelmed by their circumstances, this book provides a path forward. It offers actionable steps to cultivate daily routines, mindsets, and practices that promote radical self-care. From understanding the roots of our struggles to building habits that nurture our minds, bodies, and souls, this book is a companion for the journey toward revolutionary self-renewal.

Ultimately, this book matters because it affirms a simple yet profound truth: we are all deserving of care, rest, and healing. By bridging the gap between our struggles and our self-renewal, it invites us to imagine a life defined not by scarcity but by abundance, not by despair but by hope. And in doing so, it reminds us that radical self-care is not just a personal endeavor but a revolutionary act of reclaiming our humanity.

CHAPTER 1:
AWAKENING TO THE CRISIS

STEP 1: RECOGNIZE THE ROOTS OF MENTAL HEALTH STRUGGLES

Subsection 1.1: The Invisible Burdens
Exploring societal pressures, historical traumas, and personal neglect

The concept of invisible burdens encompasses the unseen, often unacknowledged pressures that weigh on individuals in their daily lives. These burdens, while intangible, have profound effects on mental, emotional, and physical well-being. They stem from societal expectations, historical traumas, and personal neglect, creating a complex web of challenges that many struggle to navigate.

1. Societal Pressures: The Weight of Expectations

Modern society is rife with expectations that dictate how individuals should live, look, and succeed. These pressures are especially pronounced in the era of social media, where curated snapshots of others' lives can foster feelings of inadequacy and self-doubt. The relentless pursuit of perfection—whether in appearance, career, or relationships—creates a sense of chronic insufficiency. This is further exacerbated by cultural norms that glorify overwork and equate rest with laziness, leaving little room for much needed self-care.

For marginalized groups, societal pressures are compounded by systemic inequalities. Racism, sexism, homophobia, and other forms of discrimination impose additional layers of stress, forcing individuals to navigate a world that often invalidates their identities and experiences. The need to constantly prove one's worth or justify one's existence can lead to profound emotional exhaustion and alienation.

2. Historical Traumas: The Legacy of Pain

Historical traumas, both collective and individual, leave an indelible mark on those who experience them. For communities affected by colonization, slavery, or war, the scars of the past are often carried forward, manifesting as intergenerational trauma. This phenomenon, where unresolved pain is passed down through families, can shape an individual's sense of self and their approach to life's challenges.

James Baldwin eloquently addressed the lingering effects of historical trauma, urging individuals and societies to confront their histories honestly. Ignoring these legacies, he warned, only perpetuates the cycle of pain. Radical self-care, in this context, becomes a means of breaking this cycle, offering a path toward healing and empowerment.

3. Personal Neglect: The Cost of Disconnection

In the helter skelter of daily life, it's easy to lose sight of one's own needs. Personal neglect often stems from a combination of external demands and internalized beliefs that prioritize others' well-being over one's own, especially in the global south. This neglect can take many forms, from skipping meals to ignoring mental health struggles, and its cumulative effect is a profound sense of disconnection from oneself.

Carl Jung's concept of the shadow—the hidden aspects of the self—is particularly relevant here. When individuals neglect their needs, they often suppress parts of themselves, leading to inner conflict and a diminished sense of wholeness. Recognizing and addressing this neglect is a crucial step in the journey toward radical self-care.

4. The Intersection of Burdens: Navigating Complexity

These invisible burdens rarely exist in isolation. Societal pressures, historical traumas, and personal neglect often intersect, creating a multifaceted web of challenges. For example, a person of color navigating a demanding corporate environment may grapple with both systemic racism and personal neglect, as they prioritize survival over self-care. Understanding this intersectionality is key to addressing the root causes of these burdens and finding paths toward relief.

5. The Path Forward: Awareness and Intention

The first step in addressing invisible burdens is acknowledging their existence. This requires cultivating self-awareness and examining the factors that contribute to one's struggles. From there, individuals can begin to set boundaries, challenge harmful societal narratives, and prioritize practices that nurture their well-being.

Radical self-care, as explored throughout this book, offers a framework for navigating these burdens with intention and resilience. By addressing societal pressures, confronting historical traumas, and tending to personal needs, individuals can reclaim their agency and embark on a transformative journey toward self-renewal.

Subsection 1.2: Breaking the Silence
Learning from James Baldwin: confronting uncomfortable truths

In the pursuit of radical self-care, the concept of breaking the silence serves as a pivotal act of liberation and healing. Few figures embody the courage required to confront uncomfortable truths better than James Baldwin, a writer and thinker whose works challenge us to engage with the deepest layers of our humanity. Baldwin's insights into race, identity, and personal authenticity remain as relevant today as they were in his lifetime. His fearless confrontation of societal and personal truths provides a roadmap for breaking the silences that often bind us.

Baldwin and the Power of Speaking Truth

James Baldwin's life and writings were a testament to the transformative power of truth-telling. In works like *The Fire Next Time* and *Notes of a Native Son*, Baldwin articulated the pain of systemic injustice and the personal toll of living in a world that demanded silence in the face of inequity. His ability to name the unnameable—to speak of the suffering, rage, and longing experienced by marginalized communities—made him a beacon for those seeking to understand themselves and their place in a fractured society.

Breaking the silence in the context of radical self-care requires adopting Baldwin's willingness to confront uncomfortable truths, not only in the world around us but within ourselves. Silence often manifests as avoidance: the refusal to address trauma, the reluctance to admit fear, or the inability to articulate pain. Baldwin's writings remind us that silence does not protect us; it isolates us, perpetuating cycles of internal and external harm.

The Courage to Face Internal Truths

Baldwin's essays often delve into the intersections of personal and collective identity, exploring how external societal pressures shape internal landscapes. To practice radical self-care, we must examine our own silences—those internal dialogues we avoid because they are too painful, too revealing, or too challenging.

Consider Baldwin's assertion: "Not everything that is faced can be changed, but nothing can be changed until it is faced." This insight encapsulates the necessity of confronting the truths we'd rather ignore. Perhaps it's the lingering guilt of a past mistake, the recognition of unfulfilled dreams, or the acknowledgment of relationships that no longer serve our well-being. Breaking these internal silences involves creating space for honest self-reflection, embracing vulnerability, and seeking support when necessary.

Breaking Silence as Revolutionary Action

Baldwin understood that breaking silence was not merely a personal act but a revolutionary one. To speak out against injustice—whether personal, societal, or structural—is to disrupt the status quo. For individuals navigating the journey of radical self-care, this means resisting the societal norms that discourage self-prioritization and self-expression.

In the context of self-care, breaking silence might involve:

- Acknowledging mental health struggles and seeking professional help.
- Setting boundaries with loved ones and articulating needs.
- Challenging cultural or familial expectations that conflict with personal values.

Each of these actions requires courage, and Baldwin's legacy reminds us that such courage is not born in isolation but cultivated through intentional practice. He wrote, "The place in which I'll fit will not exist until I make it." Similarly, the space for authentic self-care does not exist until we carve it out by confronting and articulating our truths.

The Role of Community in Breaking Silence

While Baldwin's works often highlight the solitary nature of the writer's life, they also emphasize the importance of community in the process of truth-telling. In *The Fire Next Time*, Baldwin writes of the "intolerable distance" between individuals that silence creates. Breaking that silence—whether through conversation, art, or activism—bridges that distance, fostering connection and understanding.

In practicing radical self-care, building a supportive community can be transformative. Sharing one's struggles and triumphs with trusted friends, family, or support groups breaks the isolation that silence imposes. Baldwin's life demonstrates that collective efforts to confront and address uncomfortable truths can create profound change, both personally and socially.

Practical Steps for Breaking Silence

Inspired by Baldwin's legacy, here are practical steps for breaking silence in the pursuit of radical self-care:

1. **Identify Your Silences**: Reflect on areas of your life where silence prevails. Are there topics you avoid, emotions you suppress, or truths you fear?
2. **Write It Down**: Baldwin often emphasized the power of writing as a tool for self-discovery. Journaling can help clarify thoughts and provide a safe space to articulate truths.
3. **Start Small**: Begin by sharing your truths with someone you trust. It might be a friend, a therapist, or even an anonymous online community.
4. **Engage with Baldwin's Works**: Reading Baldwin's essays and books can offer insights and inspiration for your journey.
5. **Practice Self-Compassion**: Breaking silence can be emotionally taxing. Treat yourself with kindness as you navigate this process.
6. **Seek Professional Help if Needed**: Therapists and counselors can provide valuable support in confronting and articulating difficult truths.

Lessons from Baldwin for the Journey Ahead

James Baldwin's life and work remind us that breaking the silence is not a one-time act but an ongoing process. It requires persistence, resilience, and a commitment to living authentically. Baldwin's ability to articulate complex truths, even when they were uncomfortable or unwelcome, exemplifies the transformative power of honesty.

In the journey of radical self-care, Baldwin's legacy serves as both a challenge and an invitation. It challenges us to confront the silences that stifle growth and authenticity. It invites us to imagine what might be possible when those silences are broken: deeper connections, greater self-understanding, and a more just and compassionate world.

Breaking silence, as Baldwin teaches, is not merely about speaking; it is about living with integrity. As we confront the truths within ourselves and the world around us, we honor Baldwin's enduring message: that liberation begins with the courage to speak.

Subsection 1.3: Mapping the Pain
Identifying patterns that perpetuate suffering

Subsection 1.3: Mapping the Pain: Identifying Patterns That Perpetuate Suffering

Radical self-care begins with awareness, a cornerstone of which is the ability to map the pain we carry. Pain, whether physical, emotional, or spiritual, often functions as a signal pointing us to unresolved wounds or unhealthy patterns in our lives. Yet, identifying and understanding these patterns can be challenging, as they are frequently intertwined with societal conditioning, personal history, and unconscious habits.

To break free from cycles of suffering, it is essential to engage in a deliberate and compassionate process of self-examination. Mapping the pain involves charting the origins, triggers, and recurring themes of our struggles, enabling us to understand their root causes and begin the process of healing.

Recognizing the Sources of Pain

Pain is often multifaceted, stemming from various sources that may be internal or external. Identifying these sources requires honesty and introspection. Some common origins of pain include:

- **Trauma**: Unresolved past events, such as abuse, neglect, or significant loss, can leave lingering scars that influence present behaviors and emotions.
- **Negative Thought Patterns**: Repeated cycles of self-

criticism, fear, or pessimism often contribute to emotional suffering.

- **Toxic Relationships**: Interactions with individuals who undermine, exploit, or harm us can perpetuate feelings of inadequacy or distress.
- **Cultural and Societal Pressures**: Expectations around success, beauty, or behavior can create internal conflicts, particularly when they clash with personal values or realities.
- **Unmet Needs**: Lack of self-care, poor boundaries, or neglecting physical and emotional well-being can exacerbate suffering.

Acknowledging these sources is the first step in mapping the pain, as it allows us to pinpoint where intervention and care are most needed.

Identifying Patterns of Suffering

Once the sources of pain have been recognized, the next step is to identify patterns that perpetuate it. These patterns often manifest as habitual responses to stress, conflict, or discomfort. Some common examples include:

- **Avoidance**: Evading difficult conversations, emotions, or situations may provide temporary relief but often deepens the underlying issues.
- **Self-Sabotage**: Engaging in behaviors that undermine progress, such as procrastination, overindulgence, or neglecting responsibilities.
- **Overcompensation**: Striving for perfection or overachieving to mask feelings of inadequacy or insecurity.
- **Dependence**: Relying excessively on others for validation, support, or decision-making, which can lead to disempowerment.
- **Repetition of Dysfunctional Relationships**: Attracting or maintaining relationships that mirror unresolved familial or childhood dynamics.

By examining how these patterns manifest in our daily lives, we gain insight into how pain is sustained and where change is possible.

Tools for Mapping the Pain

The process of mapping pain requires both structure and flexibility, as each individual's journey is unique. Below are tools and practices that can facilitate this process:

1. **Journaling**: Writing about daily experiences, emotions, and thoughts can reveal recurring themes and provide clarity. Journaling prompts, such as "What triggers my strongest emotional reactions?" or "What beliefs do I hold about myself when I'm in pain?" can guide exploration.

2. **Therapeutic Modalities**: Working with a therapist can help uncover hidden patterns and provide strategies for addressing them. Cognitive-behavioral therapy (CBT), for example, is particularly effective in identifying and altering negative thought patterns.

3. **Body Awareness Practices**: Techniques like mindfulness, yoga, or somatic experiencing help attune us to the physical manifestations of pain, such as tension or discomfort, which often correlate with emotional distress.

4. **Visualization Exercises**: Imagining the pain as a physical map—with specific regions, boundaries, and landmarks—can make the abstract more tangible and approachable.

5. **Community Support**: Sharing experiences with trusted friends, support groups, or online communities can provide validation and insight into shared patterns of suffering.

The Role of Compassion in Mapping Pain

Self-compassion is crucial throughout this process. Mapping

pain can bring up feelings of shame, guilt, or overwhelm, especially when confronting patterns that feel deeply ingrained. Approaching this work with kindness and understanding is essential to avoid reinforcing negative self-perceptions.

Kristin Neff, a leading researcher on self-compassion, highlights three core components that can be integrated into the practice of mapping pain:

1. **Self-Kindness**: Treating oneself with care and understanding rather than harsh criticism.
2. **Common Humanity**: Recognizing that pain and imperfection are universal experiences, reducing feelings of isolation.
3. **Mindfulness**: Maintaining a balanced awareness of thoughts and emotions, avoiding over-identification or suppression.

By applying these principles, we create a safe internal environment for self-exploration and healing.

Understanding the Interplay Between Internal and External Factors

Mapping pain also involves recognizing the interplay between internal and external factors. Internal factors include our thoughts, emotions, and physical sensations, while external factors encompass relationships, environments, and societal influences. Often, these elements interact in complex ways to reinforce patterns of suffering.

For example, consider an individual who struggles with feelings of inadequacy (internal) while working in a high-pressure job that emphasizes competition and perfectionism (external). Understanding how these factors reinforce each other can help identify opportunities for intervention, such as developing healthier self-talk or seeking a more supportive work environment.

Transforming Pain into Growth

The ultimate goal of mapping pain is not simply to identify patterns but to transform them. This transformation involves shifting from reactive to proactive behaviors, replacing self-defeating habits with empowering ones, and finding meaning in experiences of suffering.

Buddhist teacher Pema Chödrön offers profound guidance on this topic, emphasizing the importance of leaning into discomfort rather than resisting it. She writes, "Nothing ever goes away until it has taught us what we need to know." By examining pain with curiosity and openness, we uncover lessons and opportunities for growth that might otherwise remain hidden.

Practical Steps for Breaking Patterns

1. **Track Triggers**: Keep a record of situations, people, or environments that consistently evoke pain. Look for patterns over time.
2. **Challenge Negative Beliefs**: Identify core beliefs that sustain suffering (e.g., "I'm unworthy") and replace them with affirming alternatives ("I deserve compassion").
3. **Set Boundaries**: Establish clear limits with individuals or situations that contribute to distress.
4. **Cultivate Resilience**: Develop practices that strengthen emotional resilience, such as gratitude exercises, mindfulness, or engaging in creative outlets.
5. **Seek Professional Guidance**: Enlist the help of counselors, coaches, or mentors to address deep-seated patterns.

Conclusion

Mapping the pain is an act of courage and self-respect. It requires us to look closely at the parts of ourselves we might prefer to ignore, but it also opens the door to profound transformation.

By identifying the patterns that perpetuate suffering, we reclaim agency over our lives and lay the groundwork for radical self-care.

This process is not linear; it will involve setbacks and challenges. However, each step taken toward greater awareness and understanding is a step toward freedom. As we continue this journey, we honor our capacity for healing and our right to a life defined not by pain, but by possibility.

CHAPTER 2: UNDERSTANDING THE SELF

STEP 2: DEFINE WHO YOU ARE

Subsection 2.1: Carl Jung and the Shadow
Embracing the hidden aspects of yourself

In the journey toward radical self-care and personal growth, one cannot fully define who they are without confronting the shadow —the hidden aspects of the self that Carl Jung so profoundly explored in his psychological theories. Jung believed that the shadow represents the parts of ourselves that we repress, deny, or remain unaware of due to societal norms, personal fears, or cultural conditioning. While these hidden traits often seem threatening, they hold the potential for immense growth, self-acceptance, and transformation.

What is the Shadow?

The shadow, as Jung described it, is the unconscious part of the psyche that contains repressed desires, fears, and instincts. It is formed early in life as we learn to navigate societal expectations and determine which behaviors are acceptable. For example, a child who is reprimanded for expressing anger may learn to suppress that emotion, relegating it to the shadow. Similarly, traits that do not align with societal ideals—such as vulnerability in men or assertiveness in women—may also be pushed into this hidden realm.

Jung emphasized that the shadow is not inherently negative; it is simply unacknowledged. Left unchecked, however, it can manifest in harmful ways, such as projecting our disowned traits onto others or repeating self-sabotaging behaviors. By embracing the shadow, we integrate these hidden aspects into a more authentic and whole version of ourselves.

Why Embrace the Shadow?

Understanding and embracing the shadow is essential for several reasons:

1. **Authenticity**: The shadow contains elements of our true nature that we've suppressed. Integrating it allows us to live more authentically.
2. **Emotional Healing**: Repressed emotions and memories often reside in the shadow. Acknowledging them can bring relief and healing.
3. **Improved Relationships**: By recognizing our own flaws and projections, we can cultivate healthier and more compassionate connections with others.
4. **Personal Growth**: The shadow often hides untapped potential, such as creativity, courage, or leadership qualities. Embracing it can unlock these abilities.

Jung famously said, "One does not become enlightened by imagining figures of light, but by making the darkness conscious." This process of bringing light to the shadow is both challenging and rewarding, requiring self-awareness, courage, and compassion.

Identifying Your Shadow

To begin the process of shadow work, you must first identify what resides in your shadow. This involves paying attention to thoughts, behaviors, and emotions that feel uncomfortable or out of character. Here are some practical steps:

1. **Notice Projections**: Jung believed that we often project our shadow traits onto others. For instance, if you find yourself overly critical of someone's assertiveness, it may be a quality you've repressed in yourself.

2. **Examine Triggers**: Strong emotional reactions, such as anger, jealousy, or shame, can indicate unresolved aspects of the shadow. Ask yourself, "What does this reaction reveal about me?"

3. **Reflect on Patterns**: Recurring challenges or conflicts in your life may stem from shadow dynamics. Identify areas where you feel stuck or repeatedly encounter the same struggles.

4. **Engage in Creative Exploration**: Art, journaling, or dream analysis can reveal hidden aspects of the psyche. Jung believed that dreams often provide direct access to the unconscious, including the shadow.

Embracing the Shadow

Once you've identified elements of your shadow, the next step is to embrace and integrate them. This process involves understanding these traits without judgment and finding constructive ways to express them. Below are strategies for shadow integration:

1. Practice Self-Compassion

Facing the shadow can be uncomfortable, as it requires acknowledging traits we may dislike or fear. Self-compassion is essential during this process. Remember that the shadow is not a reflection of your worth but a natural part of being human. Treat yourself with kindness as you explore these hidden aspects.

2. Accept Contradictions

The shadow often contains traits that conflict with how we see ourselves. For example, someone who identifies as kind and nurturing may struggle to accept feelings of anger or resentment. Embracing the shadow means accepting these contradictions and understanding that they do not diminish your positive qualities.

3. Find Healthy Outlets

Repressed traits often seek expression, sometimes in destructive ways. Providing healthy outlets for these energies can prevent harmful behaviors. For instance, channeling anger into assertive communication or physical exercise can be empowering.

4. Seek Guidance

Shadow work can be deep and intense. Working with a therapist or counselor trained in Jungian psychology can provide support and insight. Additionally, reading Jung's works or engaging with communities interested in depth psychology can offer valuable perspectives.

5. Create Rituals for Integration

Symbolic rituals can aid in shadow integration. For example, writing a letter to a disowned part of yourself or creating art that represents your shadow can make the process tangible and meaningful.

The Shadow and Radical Self-Care

In the context of radical self-care, embracing the shadow is an act of self-love and liberation. It allows us to address the root causes of self-neglect, such as shame or fear, and replace them with self-acceptance and empowerment. By integrating the shadow, we cultivate a sense of wholeness that strengthens our capacity for resilience and joy.

Consider how the following aspects of shadow integration can enhance your self-care practices:

- **Boundaries**: Recognizing and honoring your needs often involves confronting fears of rejection or guilt that reside in the shadow.
- **Authentic Expression**: Embracing repressed traits can lead to greater self-expression and creativity.
- **Empathy**: Understanding your own flaws can deepen your empathy for others, enriching relationships.

Embracing the Collective Shadow

Jung also explored the concept of the collective shadow, which encompasses the repressed traits of entire societies or cultures. Examples include systemic racism, sexism, or environmental exploitation. Just as individuals must confront their shadows, societies must address collective shadows to achieve justice and harmony.

For those committed to radical self-care, engaging with the collective shadow can be an extension of personal growth. By acknowledging our participation in systemic issues and working toward change, we align our values with our actions and contribute to a more equitable world.

Conclusion

Carl Jung's exploration of the shadow offers a powerful framework for understanding and embracing the hidden aspects of ourselves. While the process of shadow work can be challenging, it is also deeply rewarding, providing insights that foster authenticity, healing, and personal growth.

As you embark on this journey, remember that the shadow is not an enemy but a teacher. By facing it with courage and compassion, you unlock the potential for profound transformation, both within yourself and in your relationships with others. In doing so, you take another step toward defining who you are and living a life of radical self-care

Subsection 2.2: Identity in a Chaotic World
Lessons from Baldwin and Peterson on personal responsibility

Introduction

In an increasingly chaotic and fragmented world, identity serves as both an anchor and a source of liberation. However, navigating the complexities of self-definition can feel overwhelming, especially when societal forces pull individuals in conflicting directions. James Baldwin and Jordan Peterson, thinkers separated by time and ideology, converge on a profound truth: the responsibility for shaping one's identity rests primarily with the individual. While Baldwin's insights emphasize the interplay of societal structures and personal agency, Peterson's work underscores the need for meaning through responsibility. Together, they provide a powerful framework for understanding identity in turbulent times.

Baldwin's Call to Authenticity

For Baldwin, identity is not merely a static label assigned by society but a dynamic process of self-discovery and affirmation. He recognized that external forces—racism, economic inequality, and cultural alienation—seek to define individuals by limiting their potential. Yet, Baldwin's vision of liberation starts with a bold assertion: the individual must reject these imposed definitions and engage in the arduous task of self-creation.

In "The Fire Next Time," Baldwin argues that freedom is inseparable from responsibility. He writes, "You have to decide who you are and force the world to deal with you, not its idea of you." This statement encapsulates a radical notion of personal agency. For Baldwin, the journey to authenticity demands a confrontation with uncomfortable truths—about oneself and the world. It requires rejecting the narratives imposed by others and forging a self-defined identity rooted in honesty and resilience.

However, Baldwin's perspective does not ignore the role of community and collective struggle. He believed that the individual's quest for identity is intertwined with the broader fight for justice and equality. By taking responsibility for their identity, individuals contribute to the transformation of society, creating spaces where others can also thrive.

Peterson's Framework for Responsibility

Jordan Peterson, though operating in a different intellectual and cultural context, similarly places responsibility at the heart of identity formation. In his best-selling book "12 Rules for Life: An Antidote to Chaos," Peterson emphasizes the importance of shouldering responsibility as a path to meaning and stability in an unpredictable world. He argues that identity is not discovered in the abstract but built through actions, commitments, and the willingness to bear the burdens of life.

Peterson's Rule 1, "Stand up straight with your shoulders back," serves as both a literal and metaphorical instruction. It is a call to face life's challenges with courage and accountability. For Peterson, identity emerges not from a passive acceptance of circumstances but from active engagement with the chaos of existence. He warns against the dangers of nihilism and victimhood, suggesting that these mindsets undermine personal growth and agency.

Central to Peterson's philosophy is the idea that identity is constructed through responsibility—to oneself, one's family, and society at large. He asserts that meaning arises when individuals take ownership of their lives, setting goals and striving to fulfill them despite inevitable setbacks. By embracing responsibility, individuals can transform chaos into order, discovering a sense of purpose that transcends the superficial markers of identity imposed by external forces.

The Intersection of Baldwin and Peterson

At first glance, Baldwin and Peterson may seem like unlikely interlocutors. Baldwin's focus on systemic oppression contrasts with Peterson's emphasis on individual agency. Yet, their perspectives intersect in profound ways, offering complementary insights into the challenges of identity formation.

Both thinkers recognize that identity cannot be outsourced to external authorities—whether societal norms, oppressive systems, or cultural expectations. Baldwin's insistence on rejecting imposed narratives resonates with Peterson's critique of victimhood. Both argue that individuals must confront their circumstances honestly, taking responsibility for their choices and actions.

Furthermore, Baldwin and Peterson highlight the importance of courage in the face of chaos. For Baldwin, this courage involves acknowledging the pain and complexity of one's history without being defined by it. For Peterson, it means standing resolute amidst life's uncertainties, transforming suffering into meaning. In both cases, the path to identity is neither easy nor straightforward; it requires perseverance, introspection, and an unwavering commitment to truth.

Practical Applications

To integrate the lessons of Baldwin and Peterson into daily life, individuals can adopt several practical strategies:

1. **Engage in Self-Reflection:** Baldwin's call to authenticity begins with self-awareness. Set aside time to reflect on your values, beliefs, and aspirations. Ask yourself: Are these truly mine, or have they been shaped by external pressures? Journaling or meditative practices can help uncover your authentic self.

2. **Take Responsibility for Your Actions:** Peterson's emphasis on responsibility reminds us that our choices shape our identity. Embrace accountability in both small and significant matters. Whether it's fulfilling commitments or admitting mistakes, taking responsibility fosters integrity and self-respect.

3. **Confront Difficult Truths:** Both Baldwin and Peterson stress the importance of facing uncomfortable realities. This might involve addressing past traumas, challenging ingrained biases, or examining areas where you've fallen short. Growth comes from confronting, not avoiding, the truth.

4. **Set Meaningful Goals:** Peterson advocates for creating structure in life by setting clear, attainable goals. These goals provide direction and purpose, helping you navigate chaos with intention. Start with small, manageable steps and build from there.

5. **Participate in Community:** Baldwin's vision of identity emphasizes the interconnectedness of individuals. Seek

out communities that align with your values and support your growth. Shared experiences and collective efforts can enrich your sense of self.

6. **Practice Resilience:** Both thinkers highlight the need for resilience in the face of adversity. Cultivate habits that strengthen your mental and emotional fortitude, such as mindfulness, physical exercise, or seeking mentorship.

Conclusion

In a chaotic world, the quest for identity is both a personal and collective endeavor. Baldwin's insights remind us that authenticity requires rejecting imposed definitions and embracing the responsibility of self-creation. Peterson's teachings reinforce the idea that meaning and stability arise through responsibility and purposeful action. Together, their perspectives offer a roadmap for navigating the complexities of identity, empowering individuals to transform chaos into order and forge lives of meaning and integrity.

Subsection 2.3: Reclaiming Authenticity
Shedding societal masks to align with your true self

Societal expectations, cultural norms, and external pressures compel us to wear masks, creating personas that align with what others expect rather than who we truly are. These masks, while protective, can obscure our authentic selves, leaving us disconnected and unfulfilled. To live authentically is to undertake the courageous act of shedding these masks and aligning with our true nature, even when it means challenging the status quo.

The Weight of Societal Masks

From a young age, we are conditioned to fit into predefined roles. Families, schools, and communities shape our behaviors, subtly (or overtly) encouraging us to prioritize acceptance over authenticity. These societal masks serve as armor, shielding us from judgment, rejection, and failure. However, this protection comes at a cost: the suppression of our true selves.

Wearing these masks for prolonged periods can lead to internal dissonance. We may feel the gnawing sense that we are living someone else's life, adhering to goals and values that are not our own. This misalignment often manifests as anxiety, dissatisfaction, or a longing for something deeper—an urge to return to our authentic selves.

Understanding Authenticity

Authenticity is the alignment between our inner values, beliefs, and feelings with our outward actions and expressions. It requires honesty, vulnerability, and the willingness to live in accordance with our true selves, even when it's uncomfortable or inconvenient. Authenticity is not about perfection; it's about consistency—being the same person in private as we are in public.

The concept of authenticity is deeply rooted in both psychological and philosophical traditions. Carl Jung, a pioneer of analytical psychology, emphasized the importance of individuation—the process of integrating various aspects of the self to become whole. Jung believed that authenticity arises when we embrace our unique identity, including both strengths and shadows. Similarly, existentialist philosophers like Jean-Paul Sartre argued that authenticity involves living deliberately, making choices that reflect our true essence rather than societal expectations.

The Barriers to Authenticity

Reclaiming authenticity is not an easy task. Several barriers often stand in the way:

1. **Fear of Judgment:** The fear of being judged or rejected by others can compel us to hide our true selves. We may worry that authenticity will alienate us from friends, family, or colleagues.
2. **Cultural Conditioning:** Societal norms and cultural expectations often dictate what is "acceptable" behavior. These unwritten rules can stifle individuality

and creativity.

3. **Perfectionism:** The pressure to meet unrealistic standards of success or beauty can lead us to present an idealized version of ourselves rather than our authentic selves.

4. **Past Trauma:** Negative experiences, such as criticism or betrayal, can create emotional scars that make vulnerability and self-expression feel unsafe.

5. **Lack of Self-Awareness:** Without a clear understanding of who we are, it's difficult to live authentically. Self-awareness requires time, reflection, and the willingness to confront uncomfortable truths.

Steps to Reclaim Authenticity

Reclaiming authenticity is a transformative journey, one that requires introspection, courage, and persistence. The following steps can guide you along this path:

1. **Develop Self-Awareness:** Begin by exploring your values, passions, and beliefs. What brings you joy? What principles do you hold dear? Journaling, meditation, or therapy can help you uncover your authentic self.
   Reflect on moments when you felt most alive and aligned. These experiences often provide clues about your true identity. Conversely, identify situations where you felt constrained or inauthentic, as they highlight areas where societal masks may be at play.

2. **Challenge Limiting Beliefs:** Examine the beliefs that keep you tethered to societal expectations. Ask yourself: Are these beliefs serving me, or are they holding me back? Replace limiting narratives with empowering ones. For instance, instead of thinking, "I must always please others to be loved," affirm, "I am worthy of love as my true self."

3. **Embrace Vulnerability:** Authenticity requires the courage to be vulnerable. Share your true thoughts and

feelings with trusted individuals. While vulnerability may feel risky, it fosters deeper connections and builds resilience. Remember, authenticity is not about revealing everything to everyone but being genuine in your interactions.

4. **Set Boundaries:** Protecting your authenticity often involves setting boundaries with those who pressure you to conform. Learn to say no to situations or relationships that compromise your values. Boundaries are not acts of selfishness but expressions of self-respect.

5. **Align Actions with Values:** Consistency between your inner beliefs and outward actions is a hallmark of authenticity. If you value creativity, make time for artistic pursuits. If honesty is important to you, practice transparency in your relationships. Living in alignment with your values cultivates a sense of integrity and fulfillment.

6. **Cultivate Self-Compassion:** The journey to authenticity is fraught with challenges and setbacks. Practice self-compassion by treating yourself with kindness and understanding. Accept that you will not always get it right, and view mistakes as opportunities for growth.

7. **Seek Support:** Surround yourself with individuals who celebrate your authenticity. Join communities or groups that align with your values and interests. Supportive relationships provide encouragement and validation as you navigate this transformative journey.

The Rewards of Living Authentically

Reclaiming authenticity is not merely an act of self-liberation; it has profound ripple effects on your relationships, career, and overall well-being. When you live authentically:

- **You Experience Greater Fulfillment:** Aligning with your true self allows you to pursue goals and passions that resonate deeply with your values, leading to a more meaningful life.

- **Your Relationships Deepen:** Authenticity fosters trust and intimacy. By showing up as your true self, you encourage others to do the same, creating relationships based on mutual respect and understanding.
- **You Build Resilience:** Living authentically strengthens your ability to navigate challenges. When you are grounded in your true self, external criticisms or setbacks carry less weight.
- **You Inspire Others:** Authenticity is contagious. By embracing your true self, you inspire others to embark on their own journeys of self-discovery and self-expression.

Authenticity in Practice: Real-Life Examples

Consider the stories of individuals who have reclaimed authenticity in their lives:

- **James Baldwin:** As a gay Black writer in mid-20th century America, Baldwin faced immense societal pressures to conform. Yet, he courageously embraced his identity, using his voice to challenge injustices and articulate truths that resonated across generations. Baldwin's authenticity not only shaped his literary legacy but also empowered others to speak their truths.
- **Oprah Winfrey:** Despite growing up in poverty and facing numerous adversities, Oprah remained true to her vision and values. Her authenticity has been a cornerstone of her success, earning her trust and admiration worldwide.
- **Everyday Heroes:** Authenticity is not limited to public figures. Consider the teacher who creates a dialogical teaching model, the entrepreneur who builds a social enterprise aligned with their values, or the parent who models vulnerability for their children. Each act of authenticity contributes to a more honest and compassionate world.

Conclusion

Reclaiming authenticity is a journey back to yourself. It requires shedding societal masks, challenging limiting beliefs, and embracing the courage to live in alignment with your true self. While the path may be challenging, the rewards are immeasurable: deeper connections, a sense of purpose, and the freedom to live a life that is uniquely yours.

In a world that often demands conformity, authenticity is a revolutionary act. By reclaiming your true self, you not only transform your own life but also inspire others to do the same, creating a ripple effect of honesty, courage, and connection.

CHAPTER 3: THE POWER OF SOLITUDE

STEP 3: CREATE SACRED SPACE FOR REFLECTION

Subsection 3.1: Solitude as Resistance
Angela Davis on finding strength in stillness

Introduction

In a world driven by constant connectivity and ceaseless noise, solitude is often misunderstood and undervalued. Yet, as Angela Davis—scholar, activist, and revolutionary—teaches us, solitude can be a profound act of resistance. It is within the stillness that we cultivate the strength to confront societal injustices, heal from personal wounds, and reclaim our sense of self. Davis's life and philosophy remind us that solitude is not an escape but a deliberate act of introspection and empowerment.

Solitude as a Radical Choice

Angela Davis's experiences, particularly during her time in prison, exemplify the transformative power of solitude. Stripped of freedom and thrust into isolation, Davis could have succumbed to despair. Instead, she used the stillness as a space to reflect, strategize, and fortify her spirit. Her writings from this period reveal a profound understanding of solitude as both a personal sanctuary and a political act.

For Davis, solitude was not merely about being alone but about creating a mental and emotional space to resist the forces that sought to silence her. She recognized that solitude could be a radical choice in a world that thrives on distraction and conformity. It offered her the clarity to envision a better future and the resilience to work toward it.

The Misconceptions About Solitude

Modern society often equates solitude with loneliness or unproductivity. Social media, work obligations, and cultural narratives perpetuate the idea that constant engagement is necessary for success and fulfillment. However, this relentless busyness can erode our sense of self, leaving us disconnected and depleted.

Solitude, in contrast, is a state of intentional withdrawal. It is not about isolating oneself from others but about turning inward to reconnect with our thoughts, emotions, and values. Davis's example challenges the stigma around solitude, reframing it as a powerful tool for self-discovery and resistance.

The Strength Found in Stillness

Angela Davis's advocacy for justice and equality required immense mental and emotional strength—strength she often cultivated in moments of stillness. Solitude allowed her to process complex emotions, confront internalized fears, and develop strategies for collective action. In this sense, stillness became a source of renewal, enabling her to persist in the face of adversity.

The strength found in stillness is not passive. It involves active engagement with one's inner world, fostering self-awareness and resilience. This process can be uncomfortable, as it often requires confronting painful truths and letting go of external validations. Yet, it is through this discomfort that growth occurs.

Solitude as Resistance in Practice

To embrace solitude as resistance, consider the following practices inspired by Angela Davis's philosophy:

1. **Create Intentional Space:** Set aside time each day or

week to disconnect from external distractions. Whether it's a quiet corner in your home, a park bench, or a secluded spot in nature, find a space where you can reflect without interruption.

2. **Practice Mindful Reflection:** Use solitude to observe your thoughts and emotions without judgment. Journaling, meditation, or simply sitting in silence can help you gain insight into your inner world.

3. **Engage with Revolutionary Texts:** Reading works by thinkers like Angela Davis, James Baldwin, or Audre Lorde can inspire you to view solitude as a means of empowerment. Their writings provide perspectives on using stillness to challenge societal norms and envision transformative change.

4. **Set Boundaries:** Protect your sacred space by setting boundaries with others. Let loved ones and colleagues know when you need uninterrupted time for reflection. Communicate that this practice is essential for your well-being and growth.

5. **Embrace Discomfort:** Solitude may initially feel unsettling, especially if you're accustomed to constant activity. Acknowledge this discomfort as part of the process and trust that it will lead to greater clarity and strength.

The Ripple Effects of Solitude

When practiced intentionally, solitude has profound ripple effects on your relationships, work, and activism. By reconnecting with yourself, you bring greater authenticity and purpose to your interactions with others. Solitude equips you with the clarity to discern what truly matters, enabling you to prioritize meaningful actions over performative busyness.

For Angela Davis, solitude was not just a personal refuge but a foundation for collective action. Her moments of stillness allowed her to articulate a vision of justice that inspired countless others.

Similarly, by embracing solitude, you can develop the inner strength and clarity needed to contribute meaningfully to your community and the broader world.

Conclusion

Solitude is a revolutionary act. It is a choice to step away from the noise, reclaim your inner world, and align with your true purpose. Angela Davis's life and work remind us that solitude is not a retreat but a return—a return to our values, our vision, and our strength.

In embracing solitude, you resist the forces that seek to fragment your attention and obscure your authenticity. You create space for reflection, healing, and growth, empowering yourself to navigate life's challenges with resilience and grace. Let solitude be your sanctuary and your source of strength, guiding you toward a life of purpose and self-liberation.

Subsection 3.2: Building a Daily Ritual
Designing habits for mindfulness and intentionality

Introduction

A well-designed daily ritual serves as a powerful anchor in our fast-paced lives, helping us cultivate mindfulness and intentionality. It's not about adding more tasks to an already packed schedule but creating meaningful routines that nurture our mental, emotional, and spiritual well-being. By building habits aligned with our values, we transform ordinary moments into opportunities for reflection, gratitude, and growth.

The Role of Rituals in Mindfulness

Mindfulness is the practice of being fully present in the moment, aware of our thoughts, emotions, and surroundings without judgment. Rituals act as gateways to mindfulness by structuring our time and giving us the space to pause and reflect. Whether it's savoring a morning cup of tea, journaling, or meditating, rituals bring intentionality to our daily lives, grounding us amidst the chaos.

Why Daily Rituals Matter

1. **Promote Consistency:** Rituals create a sense of stability, allowing us to approach each day with focus and clarity.
2. **Reduce Decision Fatigue:** By establishing routines, we minimize the mental energy spent on making trivial decisions, freeing our minds for more meaningful pursuits.
3. **Foster Self-Connection:** Rituals provide a dedicated time to check in with ourselves, fostering self-awareness and emotional balance.
4. **Enhance Productivity:** Structured habits help us prioritize tasks and channel our energy into what truly matters.

Designing a Mindful Daily Ritual

Building a daily ritual doesn't require grand gestures or elaborate plans. The key is to start small and tailor your practices to your unique needs and goals. Here are steps to help you design a ritual that fosters mindfulness and intentionality:

1. **Define Your Purpose:** Begin by reflecting on what you want to achieve through your daily ritual. Is it greater calm, creativity, focus, or self-care? Having a clear intention will guide your choices.
2. **Identify Key Moments:** Anchor your ritual to specific times of the day, such as morning, midday, or evening. Each moment serves a unique purpose:
   - **Morning:** Set the tone for the day with practices that energize and inspire you.
   - **Midday:** Pause to recalibrate, especially during stressful or busy periods.
   - **Evening:** Unwind and reflect, preparing your mind and body for restful sleep.
3. **Choose Meaningful Practices:** Select activities that

align with your goals and resonate with your values. Examples include:

- o **Mindfulness Exercises:** Meditation, deep breathing, or mindful walking.
- o **Creative Pursuits:** Writing, sketching, or playing a musical instrument.
- o **Physical Movement:** Yoga, stretching, or a gentle workout.
- o **Self-Reflection:** Journaling, gratitude lists, or goal setting.

4. **Start Small:** Begin with a simple ritual that takes no more than 5-10 minutes. As you build consistency, you can gradually expand your practice.
5. **Eliminate Distractions:** Create a dedicated space for your ritual, free from digital interruptions or external noise. This sacred space signals your mind that it's time to focus.
6. **Commit to Consistency:** Consistency is key to making your ritual a habit. Choose a time and stick to it, even on busy days. Remember, the goal is progress, not perfection.
7. **Reflect and Adjust:** Periodically evaluate your ritual to ensure it continues to serve your needs. Be flexible and open to making changes as your goals evolve.

Example Rituals for Mindfulness and Intentionality

1. **Morning Ritual:**
- o **Duration:** 20 minutes
- o **Activities:**
  - 5 minutes: Deep breathing or meditation.
  - 10 minutes: Journaling three things you're grateful for.
  - 5 minutes: Setting an intention or goal for the day.
2. **Midday Ritual:**
- o **Duration:** 15 minutes
- o **Activities:**

- 5 minutes: Step outside for fresh air or a short walk.
- 5 minutes: Stretch or do light yoga.
- 5 minutes: Reflect on your progress and recalibrate your focus.

3. **Evening Ritual:**
   o **Duration:** 30 minutes
   o **Activities:**
      - 10 minutes: Write in a journal about the day's highlights and challenges.
      - 10 minutes: Practice mindfulness with guided meditation.
      - 10 minutes: Read a book or engage in a calming activity before bed.

Integrating Rituals into Your Life

Creating a daily ritual is only half the journey; the real challenge lies in integrating it into your routine. Here are tips to help:

- **Use Triggers:** Link your ritual to an existing habit, such as brushing your teeth or brewing coffee. This makes it easier to remember and follow through.
- **Be Patient:** Building a new habit takes time. Celebrate small victories and forgive yourself if you miss a day.
- **Find Accountability:** Share your ritual with a friend or join a community with similar goals. Support from others can keep you motivated.
- **Reframe Your Mindset:** View your ritual as a gift to yourself, not a chore. Approach it with curiosity and gratitude.

The Transformative Power of Daily Rituals

When practiced consistently, daily rituals can transform your life in profound ways:

1. **Increased Self-Awareness:** Rituals encourage introspection, helping you understand your thoughts, emotions, and behaviors better.

2. **Enhanced Resilience:** Mindful habits build emotional resilience, equipping you to navigate life's challenges with greater ease.
3. **Improved Relationships:** By centering yourself through rituals, you bring a calmer and more present energy to your interactions with others.
4. **Greater Fulfillment:** Intentional habits align your actions with your values, creating a deeper sense of purpose and satisfaction.

Conclusion

Building a daily ritual is an act of self-care and empowerment. By designing habits that foster mindfulness and intentionality, you create a foundation for a more centered, fulfilling life. Remember, the beauty of rituals lies in their simplicity and adaptability. Start small, stay consistent, and allow your practice to evolve as you grow.

Let your daily ritual be a reminder that amidst the demands of life, you can always carve out moments of stillness and intention. These moments are not just pauses but opportunities to reconnect with yourself, nurture your well-being, and live with greater mindfulness and purpose.

Subsection 3.3: Journaling for Discovery
Tools to reflect on progress and challenges

Introduction

Journaling is a timeless practice that bridges the gap between thoughts and clarity. By putting pen to paper, we create a tangible record of our emotions, experiences, and aspirations, enabling us to reflect on our progress. Journaling isn't just about chronicling daily events; it's a transformative tool for self-discovery, helping us process emotions, identify patterns, and set intentional goals. In this subsection, we explore how journaling can become a cornerstone of your personal growth journey, providing practical tools to make it an effective and rewarding practice.

Why Journaling Matters

1. **Encourages Reflection:** Journaling offers a structured space to review your day, acknowledge your achievements, and learn from setbacks.
2. **Enhances Emotional Awareness:** Writing about your emotions helps you articulate feelings that may otherwise remain unresolved, fostering greater self-understanding.
3. **Boosts Problem-Solving:** By exploring challenges on paper, you gain new perspectives and uncover creative solutions.
4. **Tracks Personal Growth:** Journals act as a record of your journey, reminding you of how far you've come and motivating you to keep going.
5. **Promotes Mindfulness:** The act of journaling anchors you in the present moment, encouraging mindfulness and intentionality.

Getting Started with Journaling

Journaling doesn't require elaborate tools or techniques; the most important element is consistency. Here's how to get started:

1. **Choose Your Medium:** Decide whether you prefer a physical notebook or a digital platform. Both have advantages:
   - **Notebook:** Offers a tactile experience and a break from screens.
   - **Digital:** Convenient for on-the-go writing and allows for easy organization.
2. **Set a Schedule:** Dedicate a specific time for journaling each day. Morning and evening are particularly effective as they frame your day with intention and reflection.
3. **Create a Ritual:** Pair journaling with a comforting activity, such as drinking tea or lighting a candle, to make it an enjoyable habit.

4. **Start Small:** Begin with 5-10 minutes of writing. The key is consistency, not quantity.

Journaling Techniques for Self-Discovery

1. **Stream-of-Consciousness Writing:** Let your thoughts flow freely without worrying about grammar or structure. This technique is ideal for uncovering hidden emotions and gaining clarity on complex issues.
2. **Prompt-Based Journaling:** Use prompts to guide your writing. Examples include:
   o What am I grateful for today?
   o What challenges did I face, and how did I handle them?
   o What lesson did I learn today?
3. **Gratitude Journaling:** Focus on the positives by listing three things you're grateful for each day. This practice fosters a mindset of abundance and appreciation.
4. **Reflection Journaling:** Revisit past entries to identify patterns, celebrate progress, and gain insights into recurring challenges.
5. **Goal-Oriented Journaling:** Outline your short- and long-term goals, breaking them into actionable steps. Regularly review and adjust your plans to stay on track.
6. **Emotion Tracking:** Use your journal to explore and label your emotions, helping you recognize triggers and develop healthier coping mechanisms.

Tools and Resources for Effective Journaling

1. **Journaling Apps:**
   o **Day One:** Offers a clean interface and features like photo integration and daily reminders.
   o **Journey:** Includes guided prompts and mood tracking.
   o **Evernote:** Ideal for organizing and categorizing journal entries.
2. **Notebooks and Pens:** Invest in a notebook and pen that inspire you to write. Choose a size and style that suits your preferences, whether it's a minimalist notebook or

a vibrant, artistic journal.

3. **Prompts and Templates:** Use pre-designed templates or books with prompts to guide your journaling practice. Examples include:
   o Bullet journals for goal tracking.
   o Gratitude journals with space for daily reflections.
4. **Reflection Tools:**
   o Highlight important entries to revisit later.
   o Create summary pages to track progress over weeks or months.

Overcoming Common Challenges

1. **Writer's Block:** If you're unsure what to write, start with a simple prompt or describe your surroundings to get the words flowing.
2. **Lack of Time:** Even a few sentences can be impactful. Focus on quality over quantity.
3. **Self-Criticism:** Remember that your journal is a judgment-free zone. Write authentically without worrying about perfection.
4. **Inconsistency:** Treat journaling as a gift to yourself, not a chore. Celebrate small wins, like completing an entry after a challenging day.

Journaling for Specific Goals

1. **For Emotional Healing:**
   o Write letters to yourself or others (even if you never send them).
   o Explore forgiveness and unresolved feelings through guided prompts.
2. **For Creativity:**
   o Brainstorm ideas or sketch concepts in your journal.
   o Reflect on creative projects and set new challenges.
3. **For Professional Growth:**
   o Track achievements, challenges, and lessons learned in your career.

    ○   Set intentions for professional development and networking.

Reflecting on Progress

A key benefit of journaling is the ability to look back and see how far you've come. Make time to review past entries, noting:

- Patterns in your thoughts and behaviors.
- Recurring challenges and how you overcame them.
- Moments of growth and achievement.

Use these reflections to celebrate your journey and adjust your goals as needed.

Conclusion

Journaling is more than a tool—it's a companion on your journey of self-discovery. By dedicating time to reflect on your progress and challenges, you cultivate mindfulness, resilience, and clarity. Whether you're writing about your emotions, setting goals, or exploring creative ideas, journaling helps you connect with your inner self and navigate life with greater intentionality.

Start today with just a few words, and watch how this simple practice transforms your perspective, bringing depth and meaning to your daily experiences. Let your journal be a mirror that reflects your growth and a guide that illuminates your path forward.

CHAPTER 4: RADICAL NOURISHMENT

STEP 4: PRIORITIZE PHYSICAL AND EMOTIONAL WELL-BEING

Subsection 4.1: Food for the Body and Soul
Nutrition and its impact on mental health

Introduction

The connection between what we eat and how we feel is profound. Nutrition plays a crucial role in maintaining not only physical health but also mental and emotional well-being. A well-nourished body lays the foundation for a resilient mind, while poor dietary choices can exacerbate stress, anxiety, and depression. In this subsection, we'll explore how food impacts mental health, the science behind brain-nutrition connections, and practical steps for incorporating nourishing foods into your daily routine.

The Science of Nutrition and Mental Health

1. **The Brain's Nutritional Needs:** The brain is an energy-intensive organ, consuming about 20% of the body's energy. It requires a steady supply of nutrients, including:
   - **Omega-3 Fatty Acids:** Essential for brain function and structure, found in fatty fish, flaxseeds, and walnuts.

- o   **B Vitamins:** Vital for energy production and neurotransmitter synthesis, found in whole grains, leafy greens, and eggs.
- o   **Antioxidants:** Protect the brain from oxidative stress, found in colorful fruits and vegetables.
2. **The Gut-Brain Axis:** The gut and brain are intricately connected through the vagus nerve and gut microbiota. A healthy gut microbiome supports:
- o   Production of neurotransmitters like serotonin (the "happy hormone").
- o   Regulation of inflammation, which can affect mood and cognition.
- o   Improved stress response and emotional resilience.
3. **Blood Sugar and Mood Stability:** Fluctuating blood sugar levels can lead to mood swings, irritability, and fatigue. Balanced meals with complex carbohydrates, protein, and healthy fats help maintain stable energy and mood.

Foods That Boost Mental Health

1. **Brain-Boosting Superfoods:**
- o   **Fatty Fish:** Rich in omega-3s, supports cognitive function and reduces depression risk.
- o   **Berries:** High in antioxidants, they protect the brain from oxidative stress and improve memory.
- o   **Nuts and Seeds:** Packed with healthy fats, vitamin E, and magnesium to support brain health.
- o   **Dark Leafy Greens:** Provide folate, which helps regulate mood.
2. **Gut-Friendly Foods:**
- o   **Probiotics:** Found in yogurt, kefir, and fermented foods like kimchi and sauerkraut.
- o   **Prebiotics:** Found in garlic, onions, bananas, and whole grains, they feed beneficial gut bacteria.
3. **Mood-Enhancing Foods:**
- o   **Dark Chocolate:** Contains flavonoids, caffeine, and

serotonin precursors.

- o **Turmeric:** Curcumin, its active ingredient, has anti-inflammatory and mood-boosting properties.
- o **Green Tea:** Contains L-theanine, which promotes relaxation without drowsiness.

Foods to Limit or Avoid

1. **Processed and Sugary Foods:** High in empty calories, they contribute to inflammation and energy crashes.
2. **Alcohol and Caffeine:** Excessive consumption can disrupt sleep and exacerbate anxiety.
3. **Trans Fats:** Found in fried and processed foods, they can impair brain health and increase depression risk.

Designing a Nourishing Diet

1. **Balance is Key:** Aim for meals that include:
- o Half a plate of vegetables and fruits.
- o A quarter plate of whole grains.
- o A quarter plate of lean protein.
2. **Mindful Eating Practices:**
- o **Eat Slowly:** Pay attention to flavors and textures.
- o **Listen to Hunger Cues:** Avoid overeating by recognizing when you're satisfied.
- o **Eliminate Distractions:** Focus on your meal, not your screen.
3. **Meal Prep for Success:**
- o Plan meals for the week to ensure variety and balance.
- o Batch cook staples like grains, roasted vegetables, and proteins for quick assembly.

Emotional Nourishment Through Food

1. **Comfort Without Guilt:** Foods can be emotionally soothing without being unhealthy. For example, homemade soups or stews can offer warmth and comfort.
2. **Cultural and Social Connections:** Sharing meals with

loved ones or preparing traditional dishes can nourish the soul and strengthen relationships.

3. **Mindful Indulgences:** Treat yourself occasionally without shame, balancing indulgence with nourishment.

Overcoming Challenges to Healthy Eating

1. **Time Constraints:**
   - Opt for simple recipes with minimal ingredients.
   - Use tools like slow cookers or instant pots for hands-off cooking.
2. **Budget-Friendly Tips:**
   - Buy seasonal produce and frozen fruits and vegetables.
   - Choose affordable protein sources like beans, lentils, and eggs.
3. **Picky Eating or Food Aversions:**
   - Experiment with different preparation methods (e.g., roasted vs. steamed).
   - Incorporate disliked foods into smoothies or sauces.

Practical Steps for Integrating Nutrition into Your Routine

1. **Morning Rituals:**
   - Start your day with a nutrient-dense breakfast like oatmeal topped with berries and nuts.
2. **Midday Boost:**
   - Pack balanced lunches with a mix of vegetables, proteins, and whole grains.
3. **Evening Wind-Down:**
   - Opt for light, easily digestible dinners to promote restful sleep.
4. **Healthy Snacking:**
   - Keep snacks like hummus and veggies or trail mix on hand to curb hunger between meals.

Tracking Your Progress

1. **Food Journaling:**

- o   Track meals and moods to identify patterns and triggers.
- o   Reflect on how different foods make you feel physically and emotionally.

2. **Celebrate Small Wins:**
- o   Recognize and reward yourself for consistent healthy choices.

3. **Stay Flexible:**
- o   Remember that progress is not linear; occasional setbacks are normal and don't negate your efforts.

Conclusion

Food is both fuel for the body and nourishment for the soul. By prioritizing a diet rich in whole, nutrient-dense foods, you not only enhance physical health but also foster emotional and mental resilience. Small, intentional changes can make a profound difference, transforming your relationship with food into one of care and reverence. Let every meal be an opportunity to honor your body, mind, and spirit, fueling the journey toward radical self-care.

Subsection 4.2: The Healing Power of Rest
Unpacking sleep and restoration as revolutionary acts

In a society that glorifies productivity at the expense of well-being, rest often becomes a revolutionary act. This notion is particularly radical when contextualized within the framework of radical self-care. Rest is not merely a biological necessity; it is a profound act of resistance against a system that demands constant output and equates human worth with productivity. By prioritizing sleep and restoration, we reclaim our humanity and foster mental, emotional, and physical healing.

Sleep: The Cornerstone of Restoration

Sleep is the bedrock of rest, yet it is one of the most undervalued aspects of modern life. Science consistently highlights the profound impact of sleep on overall health. Adequate sleep strengthens our immune system, sharpens cognitive function, stabilizes emotional well-being, and supports physical recovery. Despite these benefits, many of us neglect sleep, treating it as expendable in the face of competing demands.

Cultural narratives often perpetuate the myth of the "hustle," celebrating individuals who work tirelessly with little regard for their own health. This mindset is particularly harmful to marginalized communities, where systemic inequalities frequently compound the pressure to overextend oneself. Within this context, choosing to prioritize sleep is a defiant act of self-preservation.

Radical self-care invites us to reframe sleep as sacred. It demands that we view the act of resting not as indulgence but as a non-negotiable foundation for living a fulfilled and revolutionary life. Angela Davis, whose teachings on liberation and justice deeply inspire this work, reminds us that self-care must include the care of our bodies. Rest, therefore, is not just about pausing; it is about nurturing our capacity to engage in the ongoing work of personal and collective transformation.

Unpacking Restorative Practices

Beyond sleep, restoration encompasses activities and habits that allow us to recharge physically, emotionally, and spiritually. Practices such as mindful breathing, meditation, and moments of stillness can significantly enhance our ability to rest. These practices are particularly powerful when paired with intentional reflection, enabling us to process emotions, release stress, and connect with our deeper selves.

Modern life often discourages stillness. Notifications, deadlines, and unending to-do lists create an environment where rest feels impossible. However, weaving small restorative practices into daily life can shift this dynamic. For example, setting aside just ten minutes for meditation or engaging in a brief session of yoga nidra can reset the mind and body, fostering a sense of calm and renewal.

Community-based rest practices also hold transformative potential. In her work on collective healing, Tricia Hersey, founder of The Nap Ministry, emphasizes the communal aspects of rest. She asserts that rest can be a form of resistance and communal care, urging people to come together to create spaces where rest is celebrated and facilitated. This approach not only disrupts capitalist frameworks but also fosters solidarity and shared well-being.

Rest as a Form of Liberation

Historically, rest has been weaponized against marginalized groups, particularly Black and Indigenous communities, through forced labor, systemic oppression, and the denial of leisure. In this context, reclaiming rest is an act of liberation. It asserts the intrinsic value of these communities and resists the erasure of their humanity.

Audre Lorde's declaration that "caring for myself is not self-indulgence, it is self-preservation, and that is an act of political warfare" underscores the revolutionary potential of rest. By embracing restorative practices, individuals not only care for their personal well-being but also challenge oppressive systems that thrive on exhaustion and exploitation. The act of resting becomes a way to honor ancestral resilience and contribute to the dismantling of structures that perpetuate inequality.

Practical Steps to Prioritize Rest

1. **Establish a Sleep Ritual**: Create a consistent nighttime routine that signals to your body that it is time to rest. This might include dimming the lights, reading a calming book, or engaging in light stretching. Avoiding screens for at least an hour before bed can also significantly improve sleep quality.
2. **Embrace Napping**: Short naps of 20-30 minutes can provide a restorative boost during the day without interfering with nighttime sleep. Consider building

a mid-day rest period into your schedule whenever possible.

3. **Set Boundaries**: Learn to say no to demands that encroach on your rest. Communicate your need for downtime to friends, family, and colleagues, and hold firm in protecting this time for yourself.

4. **Cultivate Restful Spaces**: Design your sleeping and resting areas to promote relaxation. This includes keeping your bedroom cool, dark, and quiet, and investing in comfortable bedding that supports restorative sleep.

5. **Engage in Reflective Practices**: Journaling, prayer, or quiet contemplation can help clear the mental clutter that often disrupts rest. These practices can also deepen your connection to your inner self and align your actions with your values.

Rest and the Inner Work of Self-Care

Rest is not just about recuperation; it is a bridge to deeper self-awareness. When we rest, we create space to confront our inner narratives, address unresolved emotions, and envision the lives we want to lead. This inner work is vital to the practice of radical self-care, as it equips us to make intentional choices and sustain long-term well-being.

Carl Jung's concept of individuation—the process of becoming whole by integrating all aspects of the self—highlights the importance of rest in personal growth. Rest allows us to step back from external pressures and engage in this transformative process. It is in moments of quiet reflection that we can begin to heal from past wounds, identify our authentic desires, and align our actions with our true selves.

Rest as a Revolutionary Mental Wellness Regimen

When we embrace rest as a central pillar of our mental wellness regimen, we challenge the narrative that equates self-worth with constant achievement. Instead, we assert that our value lies in our humanity, not our output. This shift has profound implications for how we approach life, work, and relationships.

James Baldwin's writings often explore themes of resilience and the necessity of self-examination. He understood that rest —whether through sleep, solitude, or creative expression—is integral to sustaining the spirit in the face of adversity. By prioritizing rest, we cultivate the strength to navigate life's challenges with grace and courage.

The Collective Impact of Rest

The transformative power of rest extends beyond the individual. When communities prioritize rest, they create environments where healing, creativity, and collaboration can flourish. Rest becomes a shared value that strengthens relationships and fosters collective well-being.

Grassroots movements have long recognized the importance of rest in sustaining activism. From sit-ins to vigils, the act of pausing to rest and reflect has been integral to movements for justice and equality. This collective rest fuels the resilience needed to continue the fight for change.

Conclusion

Rest is more than a personal necessity; it is a revolutionary act that reclaims our time, energy, and humanity. By prioritizing sleep and engaging in restorative practices, we nurture our capacity for healing and transformation. In doing so, we honor our intrinsic worth and contribute to a more equitable and compassionate world. Radical self-care invites us to embrace rest as an act of self-love, a tool for liberation, and a cornerstone of revolutionary mental wellness. Through rest, we find the strength to rise, the clarity to dream, and the courage to act.

Subsection 4.3: Emotional Hygiene

Managing relationships and emotional boundaries

In the practice of radical self-care, tending to emotional well-being is as essential as caring for the body. Emotional hygiene —the act of nurturing and maintaining mental and emotional health—is an ongoing process that requires intention and awareness. At its core, emotional hygiene is about understanding our feelings, managing our relationships, and setting boundaries that protect our mental space.

Understanding Emotional Hygiene

Much like physical hygiene prevents infections and promotes health, emotional hygiene safeguards us against the emotional strains that arise from unresolved conflicts, toxic relationships, and unchecked stress. Neglecting emotional hygiene can lead to burnout, resentment, and a diminished sense of self-worth.

Emotional hygiene involves several key practices:

1. **Acknowledging Emotions**: Suppressed emotions often manifest as stress, anxiety, or physical discomfort. Acknowledging our feelings without judgment is the first step toward healing. It allows us to process emotions constructively rather than letting them fester.
2. **Reflecting on Experiences**: Self-reflection helps us identify patterns in our emotional responses. Understanding these patterns enables us to make intentional choices about how we navigate relationships and situations.
3. **Engaging in Self-Compassion**: Treating ourselves with kindness when we experience emotional pain fosters resilience and self-acceptance. Self-compassion is a cornerstone of emotional hygiene, allowing us to recover from setbacks and grow through challenges.

Managing Relationships

Healthy relationships are a vital part of emotional well-being, but they require effort and intentionality. Not all relationships are beneficial, and some can drain our emotional reserves. Managing relationships effectively involves nurturing the ones that uplift us while distancing ourselves from those that harm us.

Building Healthy Connections

1. **Communicate Openly**: Clear and honest communication builds trust and prevents misunderstandings. Expressing our needs and listening to others with empathy fosters stronger connections.
2. **Invest in Reciprocal Relationships**: Focus on relationships where there is mutual care and respect. One-sided relationships, where one person consistently gives while the other takes, can lead to emotional depletion.
3. **Celebrate Supportive Communities**: Surrounding ourselves with individuals who encourage growth and healing creates a network of support that enhances emotional resilience.

Navigating Difficult Relationships

Not all relationships can be easily ended, particularly those involving family members, coworkers, or long-standing friendships. In these cases, setting boundaries becomes crucial:

- **Clarify Your Needs**: Reflect on what you need from the relationship and communicate those needs clearly.
- **Set Firm Boundaries**: Boundaries are not about controlling others but about protecting your emotional well-being. Be consistent in upholding them.
- **Know When to Let Go**: If a relationship becomes consistently harmful, it may be necessary to distance yourself or end it altogether. This is not an act of selfishness but of self-preservation.

The Power of Emotional Boundaries

Boundaries are a fundamental aspect of emotional hygiene. They define what is acceptable in our interactions with others and protect us from emotional harm. Setting and maintaining boundaries can be challenging, especially for those who fear conflict or rejection. However, it is a skill worth cultivating.

Types of Emotional Boundaries

1. **Physical Boundaries**: These involve personal space and physical interactions. Respecting and asserting these boundaries ensures comfort and safety.
2. **Time Boundaries**: Protecting our time from unnecessary demands allows us to focus on what matters most. This includes saying no to commitments that overwhelm us.
3. **Emotional Boundaries**: These involve separating our feelings from those of others. While empathy is important, absorbing another person's emotions can be draining. Emotional boundaries help us maintain balance.

Steps to Set Emotional Boundaries

1. **Identify Your Limits**: Reflect on what makes you uncomfortable or causes distress. These are areas where boundaries are needed.
2. **Communicate Assertively**: Use "I" statements to express your boundaries without blaming others. For example, "I need time to recharge and can't attend the event this weekend."
3. **Anticipate Pushback**: Not everyone will respect your boundaries immediately. Be prepared to reinforce them calmly and consistently.
4. **Practice Self-Awareness**: Regularly check in with yourself to ensure your boundaries are aligned with your emotional needs.

Emotional Hygiene in Practice

Incorporating emotional hygiene into daily life doesn't require drastic changes. Small, consistent practices can make a significant impact:

1. **Journaling**: Writing about your thoughts and feelings

helps process emotions and gain clarity.

2. **Mindful Listening**: Paying full attention to others during conversations deepens connections and reduces misunderstandings.

3. **Taking Breaks**: Stepping away from emotionally intense situations allows you to recharge and approach them with a fresh perspective.

4. **Engaging in Therapy or Counseling**: Professional support provides tools and insights for navigating complex emotions and relationships.

The Role of Emotional Hygiene in Radical Self-Care

Emotional hygiene is an act of self-respect and a cornerstone of radical self-care. By prioritizing our emotional well-being, we create a foundation for resilience, authenticity, and meaningful relationships. This practice aligns with Angela Davis's call to care for ourselves as an act of revolution—a defiance of systems that demand we sacrifice our well-being for productivity.

Emotional hygiene also supports mental wellness. Carl Jung's emphasis on shadow work—facing and integrating the hidden aspects of ourselves—underscores the importance of addressing emotions we'd rather avoid. When we confront these feelings, we move toward wholeness and healing.

Conclusion

Emotional hygiene is not a one-time act but a lifelong practice. It requires us to be intentional about our relationships, set and uphold boundaries, and nurture our inner emotional landscape. By doing so, we honor our needs, foster healthier connections, and reclaim our emotional well-being as a revolutionary act. Radical self-care challenges us to prioritize our emotional health, transforming how we engage with ourselves and the world around us.

CHAPTER 5:
BUILDING A VISION
FOR YOUR LIFE

STEP 5: CREATE MEANING AND PURPOSE

Subsection 5.1: The Myth of Sisyphus: Lessons in Struggle
Finding meaning in challenges

In Albert Camus's philosophical essay *The Myth of Sisyphus*, the Greek mythological figure Sisyphus is condemned to an eternal cycle of rolling a boulder up a hill, only for it to roll back down each time. At first glance, Sisyphus's punishment appears to embody futility and despair. However, Camus challenges us to imagine Sisyphus happy. Why? Because, in embracing the absurdity of his predicament, Sisyphus defies it. He creates meaning within his struggle, transforming an otherwise hopeless task into an act of rebellion and, ultimately, a source of purpose.

This myth offers profound lessons about finding meaning in challenges. While our struggles may not involve pushing literal boulders, they often feel equally repetitive, unrelenting, and beyond our control. Yet, as Camus suggests, it is not the challenge itself but our response to it that defines our experience. By reframing struggle as an opportunity for growth and discovery, we can transform even the most difficult circumstances into meaningful pursuits.

Embracing the Absurd

Camus introduces the concept of the absurd—the tension between our desire for meaning and the chaotic, indifferent nature of the universe. He argues that while life may lack inherent meaning, this realization does not lead to despair. Instead, it invites us to create our own purpose.

To embrace the absurd is to accept life's unpredictability and challenges without succumbing to nihilism. It means recognizing that struggle is an inevitable part of existence and choosing to engage with it consciously and creatively. This perspective shifts our focus from the external outcome of our efforts to the internal transformation they provoke.

For instance, consider the challenges of pursuing a demanding career, maintaining relationships, or navigating personal setbacks. These experiences often feel overwhelming, yet they also shape our character, deepen our understanding, and strengthen our resilience. When we view struggle as an integral part of our journey, it becomes a teacher rather than a tormentor.

Finding Meaning in Challenges

1. **Reframe Struggles as Opportunities**: Challenges often hold hidden opportunities for growth. By shifting our perspective from "Why is this happening to me?" to "What can I learn from this?" We transform adversity into a catalyst for self-discovery and empowerment.
   For example, losing a job might feel devastating initially, but it can also prompt us to explore new paths, develop overlooked skills, or realign our priorities. In this sense, challenges become stepping stones rather than stumbling blocks.

2. **Focus on the Process, Not Just the Outcome**: Much like Sisyphus's eternal task, many of life's efforts may not yield the results we desire. However, the process itself can be enriching. Whether it's the discipline cultivated through hard work, the connections forged through collaboration, or the insights gained through introspection, these experiences hold intrinsic value.
   For instance, training for a marathon might not result

in a first-place finish, but the physical fitness, mental endurance, and sense of accomplishment developed along the way are equally meaningful.

3. **Cultivate Gratitude Amid Adversity**: Even in the midst of struggle, there are moments of beauty and connection that sustain us. By cultivating gratitude, we shift our focus from what is lacking to what is present, fostering a sense of abundance and purpose.

   Keeping a gratitude journal, practicing mindfulness, or simply pausing to appreciate small joys—a kind gesture, a vibrant sunset, a shared laugh—can ground us in the present and remind us of life's inherent richness.

The Role of Resilience

Resilience is the ability to navigate challenges with strength and adaptability. It is not about avoiding difficulty but about facing it with courage and resourcefulness. Building resilience involves several key practices:

1. **Developing a Growth Mindset**: Viewing challenges as opportunities to learn and improve fosters resilience. This mindset helps us approach setbacks with curiosity rather than defeat.

2. **Building a Support Network**: Connections with others provide emotional sustenance during tough times. Sharing our struggles and receiving encouragement from trusted friends, family, or mentors reminds us that we are not alone.

3. **Practicing Self-Compassion**: Treating ourselves with kindness during periods of difficulty enhances our capacity to recover and persevere. Self-compassion involves acknowledging our pain without judgment and affirming our worth regardless of external circumstances.

The Connection Between Struggle and Purpose

Challenges often illuminate what matters most to us. They compel us to confront our values, clarify our goals, and refine our sense of purpose. For example, someone recovering from a serious illness might discover a newfound appreciation for health, leading them to advocate for wellness initiatives or pursue a career in healthcare. Similarly, an individual who has experienced loss might channel their grief into creative expression or community service, finding purpose in honoring their loved ones.

This alignment between struggle and purpose is evident in the lives of many influential figures. Consider Nelson Mandela, who endured 27 years of imprisonment yet emerged with a renewed commitment to justice and reconciliation. His resilience and unwavering sense of purpose not only sustained him through hardship but also inspired transformative change on a global scale.

Practical Steps to Find Meaning in Struggle

1. **Reflect on Your Experiences**: Journaling, meditating, or talking with a trusted confidant can help you process challenges and uncover the lessons they offer. Ask yourself questions such as, "What have I learned from this?" or "How has this shaped me?"
2. **Align Actions with Values**: Identify your core values and consider how your struggles connect to them. For example, if you value compassion, a difficult caregiving experience might deepen your empathy and commitment to supporting others.
3. **Engage in Meaningful Activities**: Pursuing activities that align with your interests and strengths can provide a sense of purpose and fulfillment, even amid challenges. Volunteering, creative expression, or skill-building are just a few examples.
4. **Seek Inspiration**: Stories of others who have transformed adversity into purpose can be profoundly motivating. Whether through books, documentaries, or

personal conversations, these narratives remind us of our capacity to find meaning in struggle.

Conclusion

The myth of Sisyphus reminds us that while life may not always provide clear answers, we have the power to create our own meaning. By embracing struggle as an opportunity for growth and aligning our actions with our values, we transform adversity into purpose. In doing so, we honor the complexity of the human experience and affirm our resilience, creativity, and capacity for joy. Finding meaning in challenges is not merely a coping mechanism; it is a revolutionary act that empowers us to build a life of depth, intention, and fulfillment.

Subsection 5.2: Crafting a Personal Mission
Jordan Peterson on responsibility and long-term goals

A personal mission acts as a compass, guiding us through life's complexities and providing clarity in moments of uncertainty. Jordan Peterson, a renowned psychologist and thinker, emphasizes the importance of responsibility and long-term goals in crafting a meaningful life. He argues that meaning emerges not from fleeting pleasures but from the pursuit of responsibility and the commitment to a higher purpose.

The Role of Responsibility

According to Peterson, responsibility is foundational to a meaningful life. Taking responsibility for ourselves and others requires us to confront life's challenges with courage and intention. While this path is demanding, it is also deeply rewarding, as it instills a sense of purpose and accomplishment.

1. **Owning Your Choices**: Embracing responsibility begins with acknowledging that we have agency over our decisions and their consequences. This mindset empowers us to take control of our lives and work toward our goals.
2. **Contributing to Others**: Responsibility extends beyond

the self. Supporting family, friends, and communities creates a ripple effect of positive impact. Whether through mentoring, volunteering, or acts of kindness, contributing to others' well-being fosters connection and meaning.

3. **Facing Adversity**: Responsibility requires us to confront difficulties rather than avoid them. By addressing challenges head-on, we develop resilience and confidence in our ability to overcome obstacles.

The Importance of Long-Term Goals

Peterson often discusses the value of setting and pursuing long-term goals. While immediate gratification offers temporary satisfaction, long-term goals provide a sustained sense of purpose. They challenge us to grow, adapt, and strive toward something greater than ourselves.

1. **Define Your Vision**: Clarify what you want to achieve and why it matters to you. A clear vision serves as a motivational anchor during times of doubt or difficulty.
2. **Break Goals into Steps**: Large goals can feel overwhelming, but breaking them into smaller, actionable steps makes them more manageable. Celebrate progress along the way to maintain momentum.
3. **Stay Flexible**: Life is unpredictable, and goals may need to evolve. Flexibility allows us to adapt while staying aligned with our overarching mission.

Practical Steps to Craft a Personal Mission

1. **Identify Core Values**: Reflect on what matters most to you—integrity, creativity, compassion, or growth, for example. These values form the foundation of your mission.
2. **Write a Personal Mission Statement**: Combine your values, strengths, and aspirations into a concise

statement that encapsulates your purpose. For example, "My mission is to empower others through education and inspire lifelong learning."

3. **Set Meaningful Goals**: Align your short-term and long-term goals with your mission. Ensure they are specific, measurable, achievable, relevant, and time-bound (SMART).

4. **Reflect and Revise**: Periodically revisit your mission statement to ensure it remains aligned with your evolving values and circumstances. Life is dynamic, and your mission may adapt over time.

Integrating Responsibility and Mission

The interplay between responsibility and a personal mission is transformative. By shouldering responsibility, we build the discipline and character needed to pursue our mission effectively. Conversely, a clear mission provides the motivation and direction to navigate responsibilities with purpose and determination.

For example, a teacher who embraces the responsibility of educating students may craft a mission centered on fostering curiosity and critical thinking. This mission not only shapes their professional approach but also enriches their sense of fulfillment and impact.

Conclusion

Crafting a personal mission is an empowering process that enables us to navigate life with intention and resilience. Drawing inspiration from Jordan Peterson's emphasis on responsibility and long-term goals, we can align our actions with our values, embrace challenges as opportunities for growth, and pursue a life of meaning and purpose. A well-crafted mission is not a static endpoint but a dynamic guide that evolves alongside us, illuminating our path and inspiring us to reach our full potential.

Subsection 5.3: Setting Revolutionary Goals
How radical purpose changes your trajectory

Radical self-care is not merely an inward act; it is the bedrock upon which transformative lives and communities are built. Setting revolutionary goals bridges the gap between personal wellness and the broader mission to affect societal change. By aligning our purpose with a radical intent, we recalibrate our trajectory, pushing ourselves beyond survival toward and significance.

Why Revolutionary Goals Matter

Ordinary goals often focus on incremental improvement—earning a promotion, losing weight, or saving for a vacation. While valid, these objectives rarely challenge us to reconsider the paradigms shaping our lives. Revolutionary goals, on the other hand, stem from an audacious reimagining of what is possible when personal well-being intersects with collective liberation. These goals inspire us to:

1. **Expand Our Horizons:** Revolutionary goals demand that we question limiting beliefs about ourselves and the world. They challenge us to envision futures where constraints are transformed into possibilities.
2. **Embrace Purpose:** Purpose is a profound motivator. Setting goals anchored in a radical purpose gives our actions greater weight, inspiring perseverance even when challenges arise.
3. **Foster Community Impact:** Unlike self-centered ambitions, revolutionary goals inherently consider the ripple effects on others, promoting solidarity and shared growth.

For instance, Angela Davis's advocacy for prison abolition wasn't about personal gain. It arose from a profound understanding that justice for all is inseparable from individual freedom. Setting goals rooted in such expansive visions ensures that our actions not only serve us but also contribute to dismantling systemic oppression.

The Psychology of Revolutionary Purpose

Psychologically, revolutionary goals tap into what Carl Jung referred to as individuation—the process of becoming one's most authentic self. When goals align with our highest values, they resonate deeply within, unlocking intrinsic motivation and fostering resilience.

Jordan Peterson's framework of adopting responsibility as a path to meaning complements this idea. Revolutionary goals demand responsibility—not just for personal success but for contributing to the greater good. This dual responsibility nurtures a sense of agency and significance, countering feelings of helplessness and apathy.

Crafting Revolutionary Goals

The process of setting revolutionary goals begins with self-reflection and extends to deliberate action. Here is a step-by-step guide to ensure your goals are both impactful and attainable:

1. **Reflect on Core Values:** Start by identifying the principles that anchor your life. Are you committed to justice, equity, creativity, or environmental stewardship? Your values will serve as the foundation for your goals.
2. **Envision Radical Outcomes:** Imagine a future where those values are fully realized. What does that world look like? How does it feel to contribute to such a transformation? This exercise activates your imagination, an essential component of revolutionary thinking.
3. **Set SMART but Revolutionary Objectives:** Borrowing from the SMART framework (Specific, Measurable, Achievable, Relevant, Time-bound), ensure that your goals, while ambitious, remain practical. For example, instead of vaguely aiming to "help marginalized communities," set a goal like: "Launch a mentorship program for 20 youth from underserved backgrounds within two years."
4. **Identify Stakeholders:** Revolutionary goals are rarely

achieved in isolation. Identify allies, mentors, and collaborators who share your vision. Building a network of support amplifies your impact and keeps you accountable.

5. **Create Milestones:** Break your goal into manageable steps. Milestones provide opportunities to celebrate progress and recalibrate strategies if necessary.

Overcoming Barriers to Revolutionary Goals

The path to revolutionary change is fraught with challenges, both internal and external. Here's how to navigate them:

1. **Combat Fear:** Fear of failure or criticism often paralyzes action. Remember, revolutionary goals inherently involve risk. Embrace fear as a natural companion to bold ambition and reframe failure as a learning opportunity.
2. **Navigate Resistance:** Systems of oppression and inertia resist change. Cultivate resilience by grounding yourself in community and drawing inspiration from historical figures who persisted despite overwhelming odds.
3. **Avoid Perfectionism:** Revolutionary work is messy and iterative. Perfectionism can stall progress, so prioritize action over flawlessness. As James Baldwin wrote, "Not everything that is faced can be changed, but nothing can be changed until it is faced."
4. **Sustain Energy:** Burnout is a real risk when pursuing audacious goals. Radical self-care remains essential. Schedule time for rest, reflection, and rejuvenation to sustain long-term efforts.

Examples of Revolutionary Goals

To illustrate the concept, consider these examples:

- **Personal Level:** Commit to organizing a weekly support group for individuals recovering from mental health challenges, promoting shared healing and solidarity.

- **Community Level:** Initiate a project to convert vacant urban lots into community gardens, addressing food insecurity while fostering environmental awareness.
- **Global Level:** Advocate for policy changes in your field of expertise, such as pushing for corporate accountability in environmental practices.

Each of these examples combines personal commitment with a broader impact, exemplifying how revolutionary goals extend beyond individual ambition.

How Revolutionary Goals Transform Trajectories

The act of setting and pursuing revolutionary goals alters not just the outcomes we achieve but also the paths we tread. Here's how:

1. **Redefining Success:** Success shifts from material accumulation to meaningful contribution. By prioritizing purpose, we find deeper fulfillment and joy.
2. **Cultivating Legacy:** Revolutionary goals leave lasting impacts. Whether through systemic reforms or personal mentorship, the ripple effects of our efforts endure beyond our lifetimes.
3. **Building Collective Power:** As individuals align their efforts with communal aspirations, the collective power of grassroots movements grows, enabling transformative change on a grand scale.

Practical Exercise: Your Revolutionary Goal

Take 20 minutes to complete the following exercise:

1. Write down three core values that matter most to you.
2. Envision one revolutionary change you would like to see in the world. Describe it in vivid detail.
3. Brainstorm one goal you can set today to contribute to that change. Ensure it is SMART.
4. Identify one person or organization you can collaborate with to amplify your impact.
5. Outline the first three steps you will take to move

toward your goal.

Closing Thoughts

Setting revolutionary goals is an act of hope and defiance. It declares that our lives—and the world around us—can and must improve. By aligning purpose with action, we create trajectories that lead not only to personal transformation but also to the liberation of those we touch. As you set out on this journey, remember that every revolutionary movement begins with a single, courageous step. The question is not whether change is possible but whether you are willing to take that step

CHAPTER 6: EMBRACING COMMUNITY

STEP 6: BUILD SUPPORT NETWORKS

Subsection 6.1: The Importance of Connection
Balancing self-care and collective care

Balancing self-care and collective care is not just a nuanced skill but a revolutionary act. In a world that often prioritizes individualism, connection is an antidote—a reminder that our well-being is intrinsically tied to the well-being of others. Embracing community allows us to ground our self-care practices within a network of mutual support and shared purpose.

Why Connection Matters

Humans are social creatures, wired for connection. Neuroscientific research highlights the profound impact of meaningful relationships on our mental and physical health. The support of a community mitigates stress, combats loneliness, and fosters resilience. Beyond personal benefits, strong social networks have the power to challenge oppressive systems, amplify marginalized voices, and inspire collective action.

Angela Davis often speaks about the intersection of personal care and collective care, emphasizing that neither can thrive in isolation. Radical self-care demands that we reject the false dichotomy between individual and communal well-being. Instead, we must view them as interdependent forces.

The Role of Collective Care in Radical Self-Care

Collective care extends the principles of self-care beyond the individual, situating them within a framework of mutual aid and interdependence. This concept is deeply rooted in traditions of social justice movements, where care has often served as both a survival mechanism and a revolutionary strategy.

For example, during the Civil Rights Movement, activists didn't just fight for systemic change—they built networks to sustain one another through the grueling realities of resistance. From organizing childcare for fellow activists to sharing meals and resources, collective care ensured that the movement could persist.

Balancing self-care and collective care means recognizing that:

1. **Self-care is a foundation:** Taking care of yourself ensures that you have the energy and capacity to support others.
2. **Collective care amplifies impact:** When individuals come together to care for one another, they create a synergy that exceeds the sum of its parts.
3. **Both are necessary:** Overemphasis on one at the expense of the other leads to imbalance. Neglecting self-care can result in burnout, while ignoring collective care fosters isolation.

Building a Support Network

Support networks can take many forms, from close-knit friendships to expansive communities united by shared values. Here are key principles for building and nurturing these networks:

1. **Authenticity:** Seek relationships where you can be your true self. Authentic connections are more likely to provide genuine support.
2. **Reciprocity:** Healthy networks are built on mutual give-and-take. Offer support as readily as you receive it.
3. **Diversity:** A diverse network—spanning different perspectives, skills, and resources—enriches your

experience and strengthens resilience.

4. **Purpose:** Shared purpose creates cohesion. Whether it's a neighborhood association, a professional group, or an activist collective, aligning around common goals fosters unity.

Practical Steps to Cultivate Connection

1. **Identify Your Needs:** Start by reflecting on what you seek in a support network. Are you looking for emotional support, professional mentorship, or collaboration on a shared cause?

2. **Join Existing Communities:** Seek out groups aligned with your interests or values. These might include local clubs, online forums, or volunteer organizations.

3. **Initiate New Connections:** Don't hesitate to reach out to others. Invite a colleague for coffee, join a conversation at an event, or message someone whose work inspires you.

4. **Foster Regular Engagement:** Relationships require consistent nurturing. Schedule regular check-ins, organize gatherings, or participate in shared activities to maintain connection.

Overcoming Barriers to Connection

Despite its importance, building and maintaining connections can be challenging. Common barriers include:

1. **Fear of Vulnerability:** Opening up to others can feel risky. Remember that vulnerability fosters trust and deeper connections.

2. **Time Constraints:** Busy schedules can limit opportunities for connection. Prioritize relationships by integrating them into your routine.

3. **Past Disappointments:** Negative experiences may create hesitation. Approach new relationships with openness and a willingness to forgive.

4. **Cultural Norms:** Societal expectations of independence can discourage reliance on others. Embrace interdependence as a strength, not a weakness.

Balancing Individuality and Community

One of the challenges of collective care is maintaining a sense of individuality within a group. While the community provides support, it's essential to avoid losing oneself in the process. Here's how to strike a balance:

1. **Set Boundaries:** Establish limits to protect your time and energy while still engaging meaningfully with others.
2. **Practice Self-Reflection:** Regularly assess whether your involvement in the community aligns with your values and goals.
3. **Celebrate Differences:** Embrace the unique qualities that each individual brings to the group, including your own.

The Transformative Power of Connection

When self-care intersects with collective care, the result is transformative. Connection not only enhances personal well-being but also drives societal change. For example:

- **Mental Health:** A supportive community reduces feelings of isolation and promotes emotional resilience.
- **Social Justice:** Collective care enables marginalized communities to organize and advocate for systemic change.
- **Innovation:** Diverse networks spark creativity and problem-solving by bringing together varied perspectives.

As James Baldwin aptly observed, "The moment we break faith with one another, the sea engulfs us, and the light goes out." Connection is both a survival strategy and a path to enlightenment, illuminating new possibilities for ourselves and the world.

Practical Exercise: Mapping Your Support Network

Take 15 minutes to complete this exercise:

1. **List Your Current Connections:** Write down the names of people or groups that currently support you.
2. **Identify Gaps:** Reflect on areas where you feel unsupported. What kind of relationships or communities could fill these gaps?
3. **Plan Action Steps:** Choose one action you can take this week to strengthen an existing connection and another to build a new one.
4. **Reflect on Balance:** Assess whether your current network supports both your self-care and collective care goals. Make adjustments as needed.

Closing Thoughts

Connection is not a luxury—it's a necessity. By weaving together the threads of self-care and collective care, we create a fabric strong enough to support ourselves and those around us. Embracing community allows us to live with greater purpose, resilience, and joy. As you build your support network, remember that every relationship—no matter how small—is a step toward a more connected and compassionate world.

Subsection 6.2: Activism and Self-Care
Angela Davis on sustaining the self while fighting for others

Angela Davis, a pioneering scholar and activist, has long emphasized the vital connection between self-care and the sustainability of social justice movements. Her work highlights an essential truth: while activism demands resilience, it must not come at the expense of the individual. Understanding this balance is crucial for those striving to challenge systemic injustices while preserving their well-being.

The Duality of Activism and Self-Care

Activism is often viewed as an act of selflessness, a commitment to others that requires unyielding dedication. However, Angela Davis reframes this narrative. She asserts that self-care is not a retreat from activism but a necessary component of it. By prioritizing self-care, activists ensure their longevity and effectiveness in the fight for justice. This duality—sustaining oneself while advocating for others—is the cornerstone of impactful, enduring activism.

The Historical Roots of Self-Care in Activism

The concept of self-care has deep roots in social justice movements. During the Civil Rights Movement, for instance, activists recognized the physical and emotional toll of their work. They created support networks, organized rest periods, and engaged in practices that fortified their resilience.

For Angela Davis, the revolutionary potential of self-care emerged from her own experiences. As a Black woman and political prisoner, she faced immense stress and isolation. Through these trials, she came to understand that taking care of one's body and mind was not a luxury but a radical act of resistance. Self-care became a way to reclaim agency, resist dehumanization, and continue the struggle.

Why Self-Care Is Essential for Activists

Activism often involves confronting systemic oppression, a task that can be emotionally, mentally, and physically exhausting. Without intentional self-care, activists risk burnout, cynicism, and even disengagement from their cause. Here are key reasons why self-care is indispensable:

1. **Sustaining Energy:** Activism is a marathon, not a sprint. Self-care replenishes energy, enabling sustained engagement over time.
2. **Maintaining Clarity:** Stress and exhaustion can cloud judgment. Practices like mindfulness, exercise, or journaling help activists remain focused and strategic.
3. **Preserving Mental Health:** Activism frequently

involves exposure to trauma. Self-care provides the tools to process these experiences and maintain psychological well-being.

4. **Modeling Change:** By prioritizing their well-being, activists demonstrate the values they seek to promote, inspiring others to do the same.

Angela Davis on the Interplay Between Self and Community

Angela Davis often speaks to the interconnectedness of individual and collective well-being. She argues that self-care and community care are not mutually exclusive but mutually reinforcing. For example, when activists care for themselves, they bring renewed energy and creativity to their communities. Similarly, when communities practice collective care, they alleviate the burden on individuals, fostering mutual support and solidarity.

In her speeches and writings, Davis highlights the importance of practices like:

- **Rest:** Acknowledging that rest is a form of resistance in a culture that glorifies overwork.
- **Reflection:** Taking time to evaluate personal motivations, achievements, and areas for growth.
- **Connection:** Building relationships within activist circles to share burdens and celebrate victories.

Practical Strategies for Balancing Activism and Self-Care

1. **Set Boundaries:** Establish limits on your time and energy to prevent overextension. This might involve delegating tasks, saying no to additional responsibilities, or scheduling regular breaks.
2. **Create Rituals:** Incorporate daily or weekly practices that nurture your well-being. These could include meditation, exercise, reading, or time spent in nature.
3. **Build Support Networks:** Surround yourself with individuals who understand and respect your

commitments. Share your challenges and lean on one another for encouragement.

4. **Engage in Joyful Activities:** Activism doesn't always have to be serious. Infusing joy and creativity into your work can prevent burnout and foster a sense of fulfillment.

5. **Seek Professional Support:** Therapy or counseling can provide a safe space to process the emotional toll of activism.

Overcoming Barriers to Self-Care

Despite its importance, many activists struggle to prioritize self-care. Common barriers include:

- **Guilt:** Feeling that time spent on self-care could be better used for activism.
- **Cultural Norms:** Societal expectations that valorize self-sacrifice and stigmatize rest.
- **Access:** Limited resources or time may hinder self-care practices.

Angela Davis's perspective challenges these barriers, encouraging activists to view self-care as integral to their mission. She reminds us that burnout serves no one and that caring for oneself enhances the capacity to care for others.

Examples of Activism and Self-Care in Practice

1. **Audre Lorde's Legacy:** The poet and activist famously wrote, "Caring for myself is not self-indulgence, it is self-preservation, and that is an act of political warfare." Lorde's words echo the sentiments of Angela Davis, reinforcing the idea that self-care is a revolutionary act.

2. **Community Healing Circles:** Many activist groups incorporate healing circles, where members share experiences, meditate, or engage in restorative practices. These circles provide emotional support and foster a sense of belonging.

3. **Restorative Retreats:** Some movements like *Kongamano La Mapinduzi* in Kenya retreats for activists, offering opportunities to rest, reflect, and reconnect with their purpose.

Practical Exercise: Designing Your Self-Care Plan

Take 15 minutes to reflect on the following:

1. **Identify Stressors:** List the aspects of your activism that drain your energy or cause distress.
2. **Recognize Needs:** Consider what practices or resources would help you address these stressors.
3. **Create a Routine:** Develop a self-care plan that incorporates daily, weekly, and monthly practices. Ensure it aligns with your lifestyle and commitments.
4. **Share Your Plan:** Discuss your self-care plan with a trusted friend or colleague. Invite them to hold you accountable and, if possible, join you in some of these practices.

Closing Thoughts

Angela Davis's wisdom teaches us that self-care and activism are not opposing forces but complementary ones. By sustaining ourselves, we ensure the sustainability of our movements. As you navigate the demands of activism, remember that your well-being is not a distraction from the cause—it is a vital part of it. Caring for yourself is, ultimately, an act of caring for the world.

Subsection 6.3: Finding Your Tribe
Surrounding yourself with supportive, like-minded people

Surrounding yourself with supportive, like-minded people is a cornerstone of radical self-care and sustained personal growth. The concept of a "tribe" transcends its traditional meaning, referring not only to shared ancestry but also to a community bound by common values, goals, and passions. Finding your tribe is about forging connections that uplift you, challenge you, and help you thrive in your purpose.

Why Finding Your Tribe Matters

The people we surround ourselves with profoundly influence our lives. Positive relationships can provide encouragement, accountability, and inspiration. Conversely, toxic or unsupportive relationships drain energy, diminish self-esteem, and hinder progress.

Angela Davis's activism highlights the importance of collective power. She reminds us that movements are built through collaboration and solidarity. In our personal lives, the same principle applies: thriving as an individual often requires the collective strength and support of a community.

Characteristics of a Supportive Tribe

A true tribe nurtures your well-being and aligns with your values. Here are some qualities to look for when seeking or cultivating your tribe:

1. **Shared Vision:** Your tribe should resonate with your goals, beliefs, and aspirations.
2. **Diversity of Thought:** While shared values are essential, diverse perspectives enrich discussions and broaden understanding.
3. **Mutual Support:** Members of your tribe celebrate your successes, offer constructive feedback, and provide comfort during challenges.
4. **Empathy:** Compassion and understanding form the foundation of meaningful connections.
5. **Growth-Oriented:** A supportive tribe encourages personal and collective development.

Steps to Find Your Tribe

1. **Clarify Your Values and Interests:** Start by reflecting on what matters most to you. Consider your passions, beliefs, and the kind of support you seek.
2. **Engage in Communities:** Join groups or organizations

aligned with your interests. This could include professional associations, hobby clubs, activist networks, or online forums.

3. **Be Authentic:** Authenticity attracts genuine connections. Share your true self with others, and seek relationships where you feel safe to do so.
4. **Initiate Relationships:** Take the initiative to meet people. Attend events, participate in discussions, and introduce yourself to others. Building a tribe often starts with small, intentional steps.
5. **Evaluate Relationships:** As connections develop, assess whether they align with your values and contribute positively to your life. Let go of relationships that drain or detract from your well-being.

Overcoming Challenges in Finding Your Tribe

Building a supportive community isn't always easy. Common challenges include:

1. **Fear of Rejection:** Vulnerability is necessary for connection but can feel intimidating. Remember that not every relationship will work out, and that's okay.
2. **Limited Access:** Geographic, social, or economic barriers may make it harder to find like-minded individuals. Online platforms can help bridge these gaps, offering access to diverse communities.
3. **Cultural Differences:** Navigating cultural norms or expectations may require extra effort. Approach differences with curiosity and respect.
4. **Past Experiences:** Negative interactions or betrayals can create hesitancy. Practice discernment, but don't let fear prevent you from forming new connections.

Cultivating Your Tribe

Once you've found your tribe, nurturing those connections is essential. Here's how to strengthen and maintain your community:

1. **Foster Reciprocity:** Balance giving and receiving support. Healthy relationships thrive on mutual care and effort.
2. **Communicate Openly:** Honest and transparent communication deepens trust and understanding.
3. **Celebrate Together:** Mark milestones and achievements as a group, reinforcing a sense of shared purpose.
4. **Practice Conflict Resolution:** Disagreements are natural. Address conflicts constructively, focusing on resolution rather than blame.
5. **Invest Time:** Relationships require consistent effort. Prioritize regular interactions and shared experiences.

The Benefits of a Tribe

Having a supportive tribe offers numerous advantages:

1. **Emotional Resilience:** A strong community provides comfort and perspective during difficult times.
2. **Accountability:** Your tribe holds you accountable to your goals and values.
3. **Inspiration:** Engaging with like-minded individuals sparks creativity and motivation.
4. **Collaboration:** Working together amplifies impact, whether in activism, personal growth, or professional endeavors.
5. **Belonging:** Being part of a tribe fosters a sense of identity and purpose.

Practical Exercise: Mapping Your Ideal Tribe

Take 15 minutes to complete this exercise:

1. **Define Your Values:** Write down your core values and interests. Reflect on the qualities you seek in a supportive community.
2. **List Existing Connections:** Identify people or groups already in your life who align with these values.

3. **Identify Gaps:** Note areas where you feel unsupported or disconnected. Consider the types of relationships or communities that could fill these gaps.
4. **Set Goals:** Choose one action to strengthen an existing relationship and another to build a new connection.
5. **Reflect:** Revisit this exercise regularly to ensure your tribe continues to meet your needs.

Closing Thoughts

Finding your tribe is a journey of self-discovery and connection. It requires intention, patience, and vulnerability but offers profound rewards. A supportive community not only enhances your personal growth but also amplifies your ability to create positive change in the world. Surround yourself with those who inspire you, challenge you, and stand by you. Together, you can achieve more than you ever could alone.

CHAPTER 7: FACING THE CHAOS

STEP 7: STRENGTHEN RESILIENCE THROUGH ADVERSITY

Subsection 7.1: Confronting the Abyss
Carl Jung and the necessity of facing your fears

Carl Jung, one of the most influential thinkers in psychology, believed that to grow and achieve self-realization, individuals must confront their fears and navigate the darkest parts of their psyche. This process, which he often described as engaging with the "Shadow," is essential for cultivating resilience and understanding one's full potential. Confronting the abyss is not an act of succumbing to despair but a courageous step toward transformation.

Understanding the Abyss

The "abyss" represents the unknown, the terrifying, and the unresolved within us. It is the accumulation of fears, traumas, and unexamined beliefs that reside in the subconscious. Jung argued that avoiding the abyss only allows these elements to grow stronger and more destructive. By facing them, we integrate the Shadow, making peace with the parts of ourselves we have long denied.

This journey is not unique to Jungian psychology. Many cultures and philosophies recognize the importance of confronting darkness to achieve enlightenment. From the hero's journey in mythology to the concept of the "dark night of the soul" in spirituality, facing the abyss is a universal path to personal growth.

The Necessity of Facing Your Fears

Fear is a natural response to perceived threats, but it can also be paralyzing. Jung emphasized that unaddressed fears often manifest in destructive ways, such as anxiety, anger, or self-sabotage. By confronting our fears directly, we strip them of their power and learn to navigate life with greater confidence and clarity.

Consider the following benefits of facing your fears:

1. **Self-Awareness:** Understanding what scares you reveals deeper truths about your values, desires, and vulnerabilities.
2. **Emotional Growth:** Facing fears builds emotional resilience, helping you cope with future challenges.
3. **Freedom:** Overcoming fear liberates you from limitations, opening doors to new opportunities and experiences.
4. **Integration:** Acknowledging and accepting all parts of yourself fosters wholeness and inner peace.

Practical Steps to Confront the Abyss

1. **Identify Your Fears:** Begin by reflecting on what scares you most. These could be external fears (e.g., failure, rejection) or internal fears (e.g., inadequacy, loss of control).
2. **Understand the Roots:** Explore the origins of your fears. Journaling, therapy, or meditation can help uncover underlying causes.
3. **Challenge Negative Beliefs:** Examine the thoughts and beliefs that fuel your fears. Are they rational? Are they serving you?
4. **Expose Yourself Gradually:** Start with small, manageable steps to confront your fears. For example, if

you fear public speaking, begin by practicing in front of a trusted friend before addressing a larger audience.

5. **Seek Support:** Share your fears with someone you trust. A supportive friend, mentor, or therapist can provide guidance and encouragement.

6. **Embrace Discomfort:** Growth often requires stepping outside your comfort zone. Accept that fear and discomfort are natural parts of the process.

7. **Celebrate Progress:** Acknowledge and celebrate each step you take toward confronting your fears. Small victories build momentum.

Lessons from Carl Jung's Philosophy

Jung believed that confronting the abyss is not a solitary act but an essential aspect of self-realization. He offered several key insights to guide this journey:

1. **The Shadow Must Be Acknowledged:** Suppressing the darker aspects of yourself only makes them stronger. Integration, not avoidance, is the goal.

2. **Symbolism as a Tool:** Jung often used dreams and symbols to explore the subconscious. Paying attention to recurring themes in your dreams or art can provide valuable insights.

3. **The Collective Unconscious:** Jung's concept of the collective unconscious suggests that our fears and struggles are part of a shared human experience. Understanding this can foster compassion for yourself and others.

4. **Individuation:** The process of individuation—becoming your true self—requires facing the abyss. Only by reconciling the conscious and unconscious parts of yourself can you achieve wholeness.

Examples of Facing the Abyss

1. **Personal Growth:** An individual with a fear of failure

might confront this by pursuing a challenging goal, learning that setbacks are opportunities for growth.

2. **Creative Breakthroughs:** Many artists and writers draw on their struggles to create powerful works of art. Facing their fears fuels their creativity.

3. **Leadership Development:** Effective leaders often face their fears head-on, whether by addressing difficult conversations or making high-stakes decisions.

Practical Exercise: Mapping Your Abyss

Take 20 minutes to complete this exercise:

1. **List Your Fears:** Write down the fears that come to mind, no matter how small or irrational they may seem.

2. **Explore Each Fear:** For each fear, ask yourself:
   o   What triggers this fear?
   o   How does it impact my life?
   o   What would happen if I confronted it?

3. **Set an Action Plan:** Choose one fear to address. Break it into small, actionable steps, and commit to tackling one step this week.

4. **Reflect:** After taking action, journal about your experience. What did you learn? How did it feel to face your fear?

Closing Thoughts

Carl Jung's wisdom teaches us that the abyss is not something to avoid but an opportunity to transform. By confronting your fears, you reclaim power over your life and take significant steps toward resilience and self-realization. The process is challenging, but the rewards—greater self-awareness, inner peace, and freedom—are profound. Facing the abyss is not the end of the journey but the beginning of a deeper, more authentic connection with yourself and the world around you.

Subsection 7.2: Transformation Through Struggle
Insights from James Baldwin on perseverance

James Baldwin, the prolific writer and activist, knew intimately the transformative power of struggle. His life and work serve as a testament to the resilience and creativity born from adversity. Baldwin's insights on perseverance remind us that facing hardship is not only inevitable but also a necessary path to growth and self-discovery. Transformation through struggle is not about avoiding pain but about using it as a catalyst for change and empowerment.

The Nature of Struggle

Struggle is a universal human experience, and Baldwin's writings often reflect on the pain of oppression, alienation, and identity. He argued that confronting these struggles head-on, rather than denying or evading them, leads to deeper understanding and authenticity.

In Baldwin's words: "You think your pain and your heartbreak are unprecedented in the history of the world, but then you read." This sentiment captures the duality of struggle—it feels deeply personal yet is part of a shared human condition. Recognizing this interconnectedness helps us find meaning in hardship and fosters a sense of solidarity with others.

Perseverance as a Tool for Transformation

Baldwin's life illustrates the power of perseverance in the face of systemic barriers. As a Black, gay man in mid-20th century America, he encountered immense discrimination and rejection. Yet, rather than succumbing to despair, Baldwin transformed his experiences into literature that challenged societal norms and inspired countless individuals.

Key lessons from Baldwin on perseverance include:

1. **Owning Your Story:** Baldwin believed that acknowledging and embracing one's truth is the first step toward transformation. He wrote with unflinching honesty about his identity, struggles, and

contradictions.

2. **Channeling Pain into Creation:** Baldwin turned his anguish into art, demonstrating that struggle can fuel creativity. Writing became a medium for him to process his emotions and advocate for justice.

3. **Seeking Connection:** Baldwin's works often emphasized the importance of love and understanding. Perseverance is not solely an individual endeavor but one that thrives through connection and empathy.

Practical Strategies for Transforming Struggle

1. **Reframe Challenges:** View struggles as opportunities for growth rather than insurmountable obstacles. Ask yourself, "What can I learn from this experience?"

2. **Find Creative Outlets:** Like Baldwin, channel your pain into creativity. Whether through writing, art, music, or other forms of expression, creativity can be a powerful way to process emotions and find meaning.

3. **Cultivate Resilience:** Build habits that strengthen your mental and emotional resilience, such as mindfulness, journaling, and seeking support from trusted individuals.

4. **Engage with Others:** Share your experiences and listen to others' stories. Connection fosters understanding and reminds you that you are not alone in your struggles.

5. **Advocate for Change:** Use your experiences to inspire action. Advocacy, whether on a personal or societal level, transforms struggle into a force for positive change.

Baldwin's Insights on Growth

Baldwin's reflections often highlight the paradox of struggle: it is both painful and liberating. He wrote, "Not everything that is faced can be changed, but nothing can be changed until it is faced." This philosophy underscores the importance of confronting challenges, even when the outcome is uncertain.

Transformation requires courage and vulnerability. Baldwin's life demonstrates that growth is not about erasing hardship but about integrating it into a more profound understanding of oneself and the world. Through this process, we gain the strength to persevere and the wisdom to inspire others.

Examples of Transformation Through Struggle

1. **Personal Narratives:** Many individuals who face adversity—whether due to discrimination, loss, or failure—find purpose and empowerment by sharing their stories. These narratives not only validate their experiences but also inspire others.
2. **Social Movements:** Struggles for civil rights, gender equality, and other causes often emerge from collective pain. These movements demonstrate how shared hardship can lead to systemic transformation.
3. **Creative Endeavors:** Writers, artists, and musicians frequently draw on their struggles to create works that resonate deeply with audiences. Baldwin's novels and essays remain timeless examples of this phenomenon.

Practical Exercise: Writing Your Transformation Story

Take 20 minutes to complete this exercise:

1. **Reflect on a Struggle:** Think of a significant challenge you've faced. Write down what happened, how it made you feel, and how you responded.
2. **Identify Lessons Learned:** Reflect on what this experience taught you about yourself and the world. How did it shape your values or perspective?
3. **Envision Growth:** Imagine how you can use this experience to inspire change or help others. Write down specific ways you can share your story or apply the lessons you've learned.
4. **Share:** Consider sharing your story with a trusted friend, group, or audience. Your journey may resonate

with others and foster connection.

Closing Thoughts

James Baldwin's life and work remind us that struggle is not the end of the story but the beginning of transformation. By facing hardship with courage and perseverance, we uncover our strength and create meaning from pain. Transformation through struggle is a testament to the resilience of the human spirit and the power of storytelling to inspire change. Baldwin's legacy challenges us to confront our struggles with honesty and hope, knowing that our journeys can illuminate the path for others.

Subsection 7.3: Tools for Resilience
Strategies to thrive in uncertainty

Resilience is the ability to adapt, recover, and thrive in the face of uncertainty and adversity. It is not an innate trait but a skill that can be developed and strengthened over time. By cultivating resilience, we empower ourselves to navigate life's challenges with confidence and grace, transforming obstacles into opportunities for growth. This section explores practical tools and strategies for building resilience and thriving in uncertainty.

Understanding Resilience

At its core, resilience involves three key components:

1. **Adaptability:** The capacity to adjust to new circumstances and embrace change.
2. **Emotional Regulation:** The ability to manage stress and maintain a positive outlook during difficult times.
3. **Connection:** Building supportive relationships that provide strength and encouragement.

Resilience is not about avoiding pain or adversity but learning to face it with courage and determination. As we develop resilience, we become better equipped to handle uncertainty and find meaning in life's complexities.

Strategies for Thriving in Uncertainty

1. **Practice Self-Compassion:**
   - Be kind to yourself during tough times. Avoid self-criticism and treat yourself with the same empathy you would offer a friend.
   - Use affirmations such as, "I am doing the best I can," to foster a sense of self-acceptance.
2. **Develop a Growth Mindset:**
   - Embrace challenges as opportunities to learn and grow. Reframe setbacks as valuable lessons rather than failures.
   - Focus on progress rather than perfection, celebrating small achievements along the way.
3. **Build Emotional Agility:**
   - Learn to navigate your emotions without becoming overwhelmed by them. Techniques such as mindfulness and deep breathing can help you stay grounded.
   - Accept negative emotions as a natural part of life, acknowledging them without judgment.
4. **Create a Routine:**
   - Establishing daily rituals can provide stability and structure during uncertain times. Simple practices like morning journaling or an evening walk can anchor your day.
   - Prioritize activities that promote well-being, such as exercise, healthy eating, and adequate sleep.
5. **Focus on What You Can Control:**
   - In uncertain situations, identify aspects within your control and take action. This can help you regain a sense of agency and reduce anxiety.
   - Let go of what you cannot change, redirecting your energy toward constructive efforts.
6. **Cultivate Optimism:**
   - Train your mind to focus on positive possibilities.

Practicing gratitude can shift your perspective and improve your outlook.

o   Surround yourself with uplifting influences, such as inspiring books, podcasts, or mentors.

7. **Strengthen Social Connections:**

o   Nurture relationships with friends, family, and community members who provide support and encouragement.

o   Don't hesitate to ask for help when needed. Vulnerability is a strength, not a weakness.

8. **Practice Problem-Solving:**

o   Break down challenges into manageable steps and brainstorm possible solutions. This systematic approach reduces overwhelm and builds confidence.

o   Evaluate each solution's pros and cons, then take decisive action.

9. **Embrace Flexibility:**

o   Be open to adjusting your plans and expectations as circumstances change. Flexibility allows you to adapt more easily to new realities.

o   Practice resilience by engaging in activities that challenge your adaptability, such as learning a new skill or traveling to unfamiliar places.

10. **Seek Meaning and Purpose:**

o   Reflect on your values and priorities to identify what truly matters to you. Aligning your actions with your purpose provides a sense of direction.

o   Engage in activities that bring fulfillment, such as volunteering, creative projects, or pursuing personal goals.

Practical Tools for Building Resilience

1. **Mindfulness and Meditation:**

o   Regular mindfulness practice helps you stay present and reduces stress. Apps like Headspace or Calm can guide you through meditation exercises.

- Begin with simple practices, such as focusing on your breath for five minutes a day.

2. **Journaling:**
- Writing about your thoughts and emotions provides clarity and helps process difficult experiences.
- Use prompts like, "What am I grateful for today?" or "How can I grow from this challenge?" to guide your reflections.

3. **Visualization:**
- Imagine yourself successfully overcoming a challenge. Visualization boosts confidence and reinforces positive outcomes.
- Pair this with affirmations to strengthen your resolve.

4. **Physical Activity:**
- Exercise releases endorphins, which improve mood and reduce stress. Even a short walk or stretching session can have a significant impact.
- Find activities you enjoy to make exercise a regular part of your routine.

5. **Resilience Journals or Logs:**
- Track your progress in building resilience by documenting challenges, strategies used, and lessons learned.
- Reflecting on past successes reinforces your ability to handle future obstacles.

6. **Professional Support:**
- Consider working with a therapist or counselor to explore deeper issues and develop personalized resilience strategies.
- Support groups can also provide a sense of community and shared understanding.

Examples of Thriving in Uncertainty

1. **Historical Figures:** Leaders like Nelson Mandela and Malala Yousafzai exemplify resilience, using their struggles as platforms for advocacy and change.

2. **Everyday Heroes:** From single parents juggling multiple responsibilities to individuals recovering from illness or loss, resilience manifests in countless forms.
3. **Personal Stories:** Reflect on your own life. Identify times when you faced uncertainty and emerged stronger. These experiences remind you of your inner strength.

Practical Exercise: Your Resilience Toolkit

Spend 15-20 minutes creating your personalized resilience toolkit:

1. **Identify Strengths:** List qualities or skills that have helped you navigate challenges in the past (e.g., creativity, determination).
2. **Choose Strategies:** Select 3-5 resilience-building techniques from this section that resonate with you.
3. **Set Goals:** Outline specific steps to integrate these strategies into your daily life. For example, commit to practicing mindfulness for 10 minutes each morning.
4. **Reflect and Revise:** Regularly review your toolkit, adding new strategies or adjusting your approach as needed.

Closing Thoughts

Resilience is not about avoiding life's challenges but learning to thrive in the midst of them. By adopting these tools and strategies, you can navigate uncertainty with greater confidence and purpose. Remember that resilience is a journey, not a destination. Each step you take strengthens your ability to adapt and grow, empowering you to face the future with courage and optimism.

CHAPTER 8: SUSTAINING THE REVOLUTION

STEP 8: CREATE A LIFELONG PRACTICE

Subsection 8.1: The Daily Practice of Radical Self-Care
Integrating routines into your life permanently

Sustaining the revolution of radical self-care requires integrating its principles into your daily life. A lifelong practice is built not through grand gestures but through consistent, intentional routines that prioritize your well-being. The daily practice of radical self-care is about aligning your actions with your values and making small, meaningful choices that nurture your mind, body, and spirit.

Why Daily Practices Matter

Daily routines create structure and stability, especially in an unpredictable world. They help reinforce habits, reduce decision fatigue, and provide a sense of purpose. When self-care becomes a routine, it is no longer a luxury or afterthought but an essential part of your life. As the saying goes, "We are what we repeatedly do." Consistency transforms fleeting moments of self-care into a sustainable lifestyle.

Designing Your Daily Practice

Creating a daily practice of radical self-care involves intentionality and flexibility. Here are steps to help you design a routine that works for you:

1. **Assess Your Needs:**
   - Take stock of your physical, emotional, and mental

health needs. What areas of your life feel neglected? Where do you need more balance?

- Reflect on your values and priorities. How can your daily routine reflect what matters most to you?

2. **Start Small:**

- Begin with simple, achievable practices that fit into your current schedule. For example, commit to five minutes of meditation or a daily gratitude journal.
- Gradually build on these habits as they become part of your routine.

3. **Be Specific:**

- Define clear, actionable goals. Instead of saying, "I'll exercise more," specify, "I'll walk for 20 minutes every morning."
- Schedule your self-care activities to ensure they become non-negotiable parts of your day.

4. **Adapt and Evolve:**

- Life is dynamic, and your self-care routine should be, too. Periodically reassess your practices and adjust them to meet your changing needs.
- Embrace flexibility without guilt. Missing a day or altering your routine doesn't mean failure; it's an opportunity to recalibrate.

Key Components of a Radical Self-Care Routine

1. **Morning Rituals:**

- Begin your day with practices that center and energize you. Examples include stretching, mindfulness meditation, or setting intentions for the day.
- Avoid immediately checking your phone or email; instead, give yourself time to connect with your inner self.

2. **Physical Health:**

- Prioritize movement that you enjoy, whether it's yoga, dancing, walking, or a structured workout.

- o   Nourish your body with balanced meals and stay hydrated throughout the day.

3. **Emotional Check-Ins:**

- o   Dedicate time to process your emotions. Journaling, therapy, or talking with a trusted friend can help you stay emotionally grounded.
- o   Practice self-compassion by acknowledging your feelings without judgment.

4. **Mindfulness and Reflection:**

- o   Incorporate mindfulness practices such as meditation, deep breathing, or mindful eating into your day.
- o   Spend a few minutes each evening reflecting on what went well and what you're grateful for.

5. **Creative Expression:**

- o   Engage in activities that inspire and fulfill you, such as writing, painting, gardening, or playing music. Creativity is a powerful form of self-care.

6. **Connection with Others:**

- o   Make time for meaningful interactions with friends, family, or community members. Genuine connections are essential for emotional and social well-being.

7. **Rest and Recovery:**

- o   Prioritize quality sleep by establishing a calming bedtime routine. Limit screen time before bed and create a restful environment.
- o   Schedule regular breaks during the day to rest and recharge.

Overcoming Challenges

Even with the best intentions, maintaining a daily self-care practice can be challenging. Common obstacles include:

1. **Time Constraints:**

- o   Solution: Integrate self-care into existing routines. For example, practice gratitude while brushing your teeth or listen to a calming podcast during your commute.

2. **Guilt or Self-Doubt:**
   - Solution: Reframe self-care as a necessity, not a selfish act. Remind yourself that taking care of your needs enables you to show up fully for others.
3. **Lack of Motivation:**
   - Solution: Focus on small wins and celebrate progress. Enlist an accountability partner to support your efforts.
4. **External Pressures:**
   - Solution: Set boundaries to protect your self-care time. Communicate your needs clearly to those around you.

Building Self-Care into Your Identity

To sustain a lifelong practice, self-care must become part of your identity. This involves shifting your mindset from "I do self-care" to "I am someone who values and practices self-care." Here are ways to reinforce this identity:

- **Affirm Your Commitment:** Use affirmations such as, "I deserve to prioritize my well-being," or "Caring for myself is a revolutionary act."
- **Surround Yourself with Support:** Engage with communities or groups that share your commitment to self-care and personal growth.
- **Celebrate Your Efforts:** Acknowledge the progress you've made, no matter how small. Self-care is a journey, not a destination.

Practical Exercise: Crafting Your Self-Care Plan

Take 15-20 minutes to create your personalized self-care plan:

1. **List Your Needs:** Identify physical, emotional, mental, and social needs that require attention.
2. **Choose Daily Practices:** Select 3-5 practices from the key components listed earlier that resonate with you.
3. **Set Intentions:** Write a brief statement summarizing your commitment to self-care. For example, "I will

prioritize my well-being by practicing gratitude, staying active, and connecting with loved ones daily."

4. **Create a Schedule:** Determine when and how you will integrate these practices into your day.
5. **Reflect Weekly:** Set aside time to review your self-care plan and make adjustments as needed.

Closing Thoughts

The daily practice of radical self-care is a lifelong journey of nurturing your well-being and honoring your values. By integrating intentional routines into your life, you create a foundation for resilience, joy, and purpose. Remember that self-care is not a destination but an ongoing process. Each small act of care reinforces your commitment to living authentically and thriving in every aspect of your life.

Subsection 8.2: Self-Care as a Political Act
Living out the legacy of Angela Davis in everyday choices

Radical self-care is not merely an act of personal well-being; it is also a profound political statement. As Angela Davis and many other activists have taught us, taking care of oneself while fighting for justice is an essential part of sustaining both the self and the movement. Self-care as a political act transforms everyday choices into deliberate actions that challenge systemic oppression, resist burnout, and reaffirm one's right to thrive.

Angela Davis and the Roots of Revolutionary Self-Care

Angela Davis's legacy is one of resilience, intellectual rigor, and unyielding commitment to social justice. Throughout her activism, she emphasized the importance of sustaining oneself while engaging in the arduous work of fighting for others. Davis's perspective on self-care emerged from the recognition that systemic oppression not only seeks to exploit and marginalize but also to exhaust and break the spirits of those who resist it.

In her speeches and writings, Davis highlighted how acts of self-preservation—from maintaining mental health to embracing joy—are inherently revolutionary. By caring for ourselves, we resist the dehumanizing forces that would have us believe we are undeserving of rest, nourishment, or fulfillment. Instead, we assert our dignity and our right to exist wholly and unapologetically.

The Intersection of Self-Care and Activism

Living out the legacy of Angela Davis involves integrating self-care into our activism and everyday lives. This integration recognizes that self-care and collective care are not separate; they are intertwined. Here's how self-care becomes a political act:

1. **Challenging Oppressive Norms:**
   - Capitalism often glorifies overwork, measuring worth by productivity. By prioritizing rest and self-care, we reject these exploitative ideals and affirm our humanity.
   - Embracing self-care disrupts societal narratives that marginalize certain groups, such as women, LGBTQ+ individuals, and people of color, by asserting their right to prioritize themselves.
2. **Sustaining the Fight for Justice:**
   - Movements for change require stamina and resilience. Activists who neglect their well-being risk burnout, which can hinder progress. Self-care ensures we remain effective in the long term.
   - Taking time to recharge enables us to approach challenges with clarity, creativity, and strength.
3. **Creating Space for Joy and Healing:**
   - In oppressive systems, joy can be an act of resistance. Celebrating life, culture, and community becomes a way to reclaim agency and cultivate hope.
   - Healing from trauma—whether personal or collective—is a necessary step in breaking cycles of oppression and envisioning new possibilities.

Everyday Choices as Political Acts

Self-care as a political act is not limited to grand gestures. It manifests in the choices we make daily, from how we allocate our time to how we engage with others. Here are ways to embody this practice:

1. **Prioritize Rest and Recovery:**
   - Rest is a revolutionary act in a society that devalues it. Allow yourself to sleep, relax, and recharge without guilt.
   - Create boundaries around your time to protect your energy and mental health.
2. **Practice Mindful Consumption:**
   - Be intentional about the media, food, and products you consume. Support businesses and creators who align with your values.
   - Limit exposure to toxic environments, whether online or offline, that drain your energy or perpetuate negativity.
3. **Cultivate Community:**
   - Surround yourself with individuals who uplift and inspire you. A strong support network fosters resilience and shared accountability for self-care.
   - Engage in collective care practices, such as mutual aid, where communities come together to support one another's needs.
4. **Engage in Advocacy:**
   - Use your voice to advocate for policies and practices that promote well-being, such as accessible healthcare, mental health resources, and workplace protections.
   - Volunteer your time or resources to organizations that align with your vision of justice and equity.

Navigating the Tensions Between Self-Care and Obligation

For many, especially those from marginalized communities, prioritizing self-care can feel selfish or indulgent. Cultural, familial, or societal pressures often place others' needs above our own. Navigating these tensions requires reframing self-care as not just an individual responsibility but a collective benefit:

1. **Reframe Guilt as Empowerment:**
   - Recognize that by caring for yourself, you model healthy practices for others and contribute to a culture of well-being.
   - Understand that your well-being is essential to fulfilling your obligations and making a meaningful impact.
2. **Set and Communicate Boundaries:**
   - Establish limits to protect your time and energy. Communicate these boundaries with clarity and compassion.
   - Remember that saying "no" to overcommitment is saying "yes" to sustainability and effectiveness.
3. **Integrate Self-Care into Service:**
   - Find ways to care for yourself while caring for others. For example, cooking a healthy meal can nourish both you and your family.
   - Seek opportunities where your passions align with acts of service, creating a synergy between personal fulfillment and collective good.

Practical Exercise: Embodying Self-Care as a Political Act

Take a moment to reflect on how your self-care practices align with your values and contribute to a broader vision of justice. Consider the following steps:

1. **Identify Your Values:**
   - Write down three core values that guide your life. Examples might include compassion, equity, or resilience.
2. **Align Your Actions:**
   - List specific self-care practices that reflect these values. For instance, if equity is a value, you might commit to supporting local businesses owned by marginalized

groups.

3. **Set Intentional Goals:**
   - Choose one action you can take this week to embody self-care as a political act. This might involve setting a boundary, joining a community initiative, or prioritizing rest.
4. **Reflect and Adjust:**
   - At the end of the week, evaluate how this action impacted your well-being and your alignment with your values. Make adjustments as needed.

The Ripple Effect of Radical Self-Care

When we embrace self-care as a political act, we inspire others to do the same. Our choices create ripples, influencing those around us and contributing to a culture that values well-being and justice. By living out the legacy of Angela Davis, we affirm that self-care is not only an individual act but a collective responsibility. It is a declaration of our worth and a commitment to building a world where everyone can thrive.

Closing Thoughts

Self-care as a political act is both a privilege and a responsibility. It requires us to confront the systems that seek to deplete us and to assert our right to rest, heal, and grow. By making self-care a central part of our lives, we honor the legacies of those who have fought for our ability to do so and pave the way for future generations to live with dignity, joy, and freedom.

Subsection 8.3: Passing It Forward
Inspiring others to embark on their own self-care journey

The transformative power of radical self-care does not end with the self; it becomes even more profound when shared with others. Inspiring others to embark on their own self-care journey creates a ripple effect, fostering resilience, empowerment, and healing across communities. Passing it forward is about more than encouragement; it's about cultivating a culture of care that uplifts everyone it touches.

The Power of Leading by Example

One of the most effective ways to inspire others is by embodying the principles of self-care in your own life. Your commitment to self-care serves as a living testament to its benefits. Here's how:

1. **Authenticity Matters:**
   - People are inspired by authenticity. When they see you prioritizing your well-being, setting boundaries, and living in alignment with your values, they're more likely to consider doing the same.
2. **Modeling Healthy Practices:**
   - Demonstrate self-care practices openly. Share your routines, discuss your challenges, and celebrate your successes. Whether it's carving out time for mindfulness or saying no to overcommitment, your actions can normalize self-care for others.
3. **Sharing Your Story:**
   - Personal stories have immense power. By sharing your journey—including the struggles, breakthroughs, and lessons—you provide a relatable narrative that encourages others to reflect on their own paths.

Building a Culture of Care

Creating a supportive environment where self-care is celebrated and encouraged is crucial for collective well-being. Here are some ways to build this culture:

1. **Open Conversations:**
   - Normalize discussions about mental health, self-care, and boundaries. Creating space for honest dialogue reduces stigma and invites others to share their experiences.
2. **Celebrate Efforts:**
   - Acknowledge and celebrate acts of self-care, both big and small. Whether it's a friend taking a mental health

day or a colleague setting boundaries, recognition reinforces positive behaviors.

3. **Encourage Collective Care:**
   o   Self-care is not just an individual responsibility; it's a collective one. Encourage mutual support within families, workplaces, and communities to create a shared foundation of care.

Practical Ways to Inspire Others

Inspiration can take many forms, from simple conversations to organized initiatives. Here are actionable ways to encourage others to prioritize self-care:

1. **Host Workshops or Gatherings:**
   o   Organize events focused on self-care practices, such as mindfulness sessions, wellness talks, or journaling workshops. These gatherings provide a platform for learning and connection.
2. **Share Resources:**
   o   Share books, articles, podcasts, or apps that have helped you on your journey. Tailor your recommendations to the needs and interests of those you're inspiring.
3. **Be a Supportive Ally:**
   o   Offer encouragement and support to those exploring self-care. Sometimes, just being a listening ear or a source of motivation can make all the difference.
4. **Leverage Social Media:**
   o   Use social platforms to share your self-care practices and insights. Your posts can reach a wide audience, sparking inspiration in unexpected places.

Mentorship and Peer Support

Mentorship is a powerful way to pass forward the principles of self-care. By guiding others through their journeys, you create lasting impact. Here's how to be an effective mentor:

1. **Listen Actively:**

o   Understand the unique challenges and goals of those you're mentoring. Tailor your guidance to meet their specific needs.

2. **Share Tools and Strategies:**

o   Provide practical advice and tools that have worked for you. Encourage experimentation so they can discover what resonates with them.

3. **Foster Independence:**

o   Empower others to take ownership of their self-care journeys. Offer guidance, but also encourage self-reflection and decision-making.

4. **Celebrate Progress:**

o   Recognize and celebrate milestones, no matter how small. Positive reinforcement fosters confidence and motivation.

Addressing Resistance and Challenges

Encouraging others to embrace self-care isn't always straightforward. Resistance can stem from cultural norms, internalized guilt, or systemic barriers. Here's how to navigate these challenges:

1. **Understand Their Perspective:**

o   Approach resistance with empathy. Understand the underlying reasons and address them with compassion.

2. **Challenge Misconceptions:**

o   Gently counter myths about self-care, such as the idea that it's selfish or indulgent, unAfrican or not manly. Share insights that highlight its necessity and benefits.

3. **Offer Practical Solutions:**

o   Help others identify small, manageable steps they can take. Overcoming initial barriers often leads to greater willingness to embrace self-care.

4. **Acknowledge Systemic Barriers:**

o   Recognize that not everyone has equal access to

self-care resources. Advocate for systemic changes that make self-care more accessible and inclusive.

Practical Exercise: Inspiring Others Through Action

Take a moment to reflect on how you can inspire someone in your life to begin their self-care journey. Follow these steps:

1. **Identify Someone Who Might Benefit:**
   - Think of a friend, family member, or colleague who could benefit from prioritizing self-care.
2. **Start a Conversation:**
   - Reach out to them and share your own experiences with self-care. Ask open-ended questions to understand their perspective.
3. **Offer a Simple Suggestion:**
   - Recommend one small action they can take, such as setting aside five minutes for deep breathing or journaling.
4. **Follow Up:**
   - Check in with them after a week to see how they're feeling. Offer encouragement and additional suggestions if needed.

The Legacy of Passing It Forward

When you inspire others to embark on their self-care journey, you contribute to a larger movement of healing and empowerment. The ripple effect of your actions can reach far beyond what you might imagine, touching lives and communities in profound ways. By passing it forward, you honor the transformative power of self-care and ensure its benefits extend to future generations.

Closing Thoughts

Passing it forward is an act of generosity, compassion, and hope. It reinforces the interconnectedness of our well-being, of ubuntu, and reminds us that self-care is not a solitary pursuit but a shared responsibility. As you inspire others to embark on their journeys, you contribute to a culture of care that uplifts us all. Together, we can create a world where self-care is not only celebrated but embraced as a vital part of our collective humanity.

Conclusion: A New Beginning

The journey from suffering to empowerment

The journey from suffering to empowerment is neither linear nor easy, but it is transformative. Along this path, you have faced the chaos within and without, explored the depths of your soul, and emerged stronger, more resilient, and more attuned to your purpose. This is not the end of the road but the beginning of a new chapter—one defined by radical self-care, intentional living, and collective empowerment.

Reflecting on the Journey

Looking back, the moments of suffering and adversity were not roadblocks but stepping stones. Each challenge presented an opportunity to learn, grow, and refine your understanding of who you are and what you stand for. By embracing these struggles, you discovered the strength to confront your fears, build resilience, and create a life rooted in authenticity and purpose.

Through self-care, you reclaimed your agency and prioritized your well-being in a world that often demands relentless productivity. By setting revolutionary goals, you aligned your actions with your values, making every step purposeful. By building supportive communities, you fostered connections that uplift and sustain you. And by facing adversity head-on, you transformed pain into power.

Empowerment Through Radical Self-Care

Empowerment is not a destination; it's a continuous process. Radical self-care equips you with the tools to navigate life's uncertainties and challenges while staying grounded in your values. It reminds you that taking care of yourself is not an act of selfishness but an act of revolution. By prioritizing your well-being, you challenge societal norms that devalue rest, reflection, and healing.

The practices you've cultivated are now part of your daily life, guiding your decisions and interactions. These routines are not rigid rules but flexible frameworks that adapt to your evolving needs. They empower you to show up fully for yourself and others, creating a ripple effect of care and compassion.

A Call to Action

As you move forward, consider how you can extend this transformation beyond yourself. How can you inspire others to embark on their journeys of radical self-care? How can you contribute to a culture that values and uplifts collective well-being? Passing it forward, as discussed, is a powerful way to ensure that the lessons and practices you've embraced continue to impact others.

Remember, your journey is part of a larger movement. Every act of self-care, every boundary set, and every moment of rest contributes to a world where well-being is a right, not a privilege. Together, we can create communities that honor the interconnectedness of our struggles and triumphs.

The Road Ahead

The road ahead is filled with possibility. Armed with the insights and tools you've gained, you are ready to face whatever comes your way with courage and grace. Life will continue to present challenges, but you now have the resilience and perspective to navigate them with strength and clarity.

Embrace this new beginning with an open heart and a steadfast commitment to your well-being. Celebrate the progress you've made, honor the lessons you've learned, and look forward to the possibilities that lie ahead. This is your time to thrive, to inspire, and to create a life that reflects the fullness of who you are.

Closing Words

In the words of James Baldwin, "Not everything that is faced can be changed, but nothing can be changed until it is faced." You have faced your fears, embraced your strengths, and embarked on a journey of radical transformation. Now, as you step into this new beginning, know that you are not alone. You are part of a community, a movement, and a legacy of empowerment.

This is your new beginning. Embrace it fully. Live it boldly. Pass it forward.

The transformative power of radical self-care

Radical self-care is not merely a set of practices; it is a profound shift in perspective that redefines how you engage with yourself and the world. It's an act of resistance against a culture that often prioritizes productivity over well-being, and it's a commitment to living with intention and authenticity. The transformative power of radical self-care lies in its ability to heal, empower, and create lasting change—both within and beyond the self.

The Essence of Radical Self-Care

At its core, radical self-care is about recognizing your inherent worth and treating yourself with the kindness, respect, and attention you deserve. It's about breaking free from societal norms that equate self-sacrifice with virtue and embracing practices that nourish your mind, body, and spirit.

Through this journey, you've learned to prioritize your well-being, set boundaries, and confront the fears and habits that once held you back. These are not just acts of care; they are acts of revolution. They challenge deeply ingrained narratives and pave the way for a more compassionate, equitable world.

A Catalyst for Transformation

The impact of radical self-care extends far beyond the individual. As you've experienced, taking care of yourself creates a ripple effect that influences your relationships, your community, and your environment. When you show up for yourself, you're better equipped to show up for others. When you model self-care, you inspire those around you to consider their own well-being.

This transformation is not limited to personal growth; it's also a call to action. Radical self-care reminds us that our choices matter, that our actions have the power to disrupt harmful systems and create spaces where everyone can thrive. It's a practice rooted in justice, equity, and the belief that every individual deserves a life of dignity and fulfillment.

Living the Legacy

As you embrace radical self-care, you join a lineage of thinkers, activists, and change-makers who have championed the idea that caring for oneself is an essential part of caring for the world. Figures like Angela Davis have shown us that self-care is not a retreat from responsibility but a foundation for sustained action. It's about building the strength and resilience needed to face life's challenges with courage and conviction.

Your commitment to self-care is a continuation of this legacy. It's a declaration that your well-being matters, that your life is valuable, and that you have the right to live with purpose and joy. By integrating these practices into your daily life, you honor those who have paved the way and contribute to a future where self-care is accessible and celebrated.

The Path Forward

As you step into this new beginning, remember that radical self-care is not a destination but a journey. It's a practice that evolves with you, adapting to your needs and circumstances. There will be moments of challenge and moments of triumph, and both are essential parts of the process.

Continue to approach this journey with curiosity, compassion, and an open heart. Celebrate your progress, learn from your setbacks, and stay committed to the practices that nurture your growth. Surround yourself with supportive communities, share your experiences, and inspire others to embark on their own paths of self-care.

Closing Reflections

The transformative power of radical self-care lies in its ability to reconnect us with our humanity. It reminds us that we are not defined by our struggles but by how we choose to navigate them. It teaches us that healing is possible, that growth is inevitable, and that empowerment begins from within.

This is your new beginning. Embrace it fully, live it boldly, and carry forward the lessons and practices that have brought you here. In doing so, you not only transform your own life but contribute to a world where radical self-care is a shared reality for all.

A call to action for readers to be both custodians of their well-being and contributors to a better world

Radical self-care is more than a personal journey; it's a call to action to transform not only your life but also the world around you. By prioritizing your well-being, you become a custodian of your own health and happiness. At the same time, you gain the strength and clarity needed to contribute to a collective vision of justice, equity, and compassion. This dual role—caring for yourself and uplifting others—is the essence of a revolutionary life.

Be a Custodian of Your Well-Being

Taking ownership of your well-being requires ongoing effort and intention. It means staying attuned to your needs, setting boundaries, and cultivating practices that sustain you. It's about making choices that honor your values and your humanity, even in the face of external pressures.

You've already laid the groundwork by embracing the principles and practices of radical self-care. Now, your task is to continue refining these habits, adapting them to life's changes, and recognizing that your self-care journey is an evolving process. Treat yourself with kindness and patience as you navigate this path. Remember that every step you take toward caring for yourself is also a step toward creating a better world.

Contribute to a Better World

The power of radical self-care lies in its ripple effects. When you invest in your well-being, you radiate strength, resilience, and compassion—qualities that inspire and uplift others. Your commitment to self-care sets an example for those around you, showing that it's possible to thrive while also working toward a greater good.

This is your opportunity to extend the impact of your journey. Engage with your community, share your story, and support others in their self-care practices. Advocate for systems and structures that prioritize collective well-being. Whether through small, everyday actions or larger initiatives, your contributions matter. They are part of a larger movement to create a world where everyone has the resources and support they need to thrive.

A Collective Vision

Imagine a world where self-care is not a luxury but a universal right. A world where individuals are empowered to care for themselves and each other, where communities are built on mutual respect and support, and where systems are designed to nurture rather than exploit. This vision begins with you.

Your journey of radical self-care has equipped you with the tools and insights needed to be a force for change. By integrating these lessons into your life and sharing them with others, you help to create a culture that values well-being as a cornerstone of justice and equity. This is the legacy of radical self-care—a legacy that you are now part of.

A Final Call to Action

As you move forward, consider these questions: How can you continue to care for yourself in ways that empower you to contribute to the world? How can your actions inspire and uplift others? How can you join forces with like-minded individuals to create a collective impact?

The answers to these questions will guide your next steps. Whether you're advocating for change, supporting a friend, or simply showing up for yourself each day, know that your efforts are meaningful. They are part of a larger story—a story of resilience, transformation, and hope.

Closing Reflections

This is not the end of your journey but a new beginning. You are now equipped with the knowledge, tools, and community to continue growing, healing, and contributing. Embrace this role as both a custodian of your well-being and a contributor to a better world. The path ahead may not always be easy, but it is filled with purpose and possibility.

Thank you for embarking on this journey. May it inspire you to live boldly, care deeply, and create a life that reflects the best of who you are. Together, we can build a world where radical self-care is not just an individual choice but a collective reality.